AGENT ORANGE AND BIOPOLITICS

A Field of Discursive Silence

SE GUN SONG

Published by Channel Asiana

First edition, 2026

ISBN: 978-1-7645718-0-7

The views expressed in this book are solely those of the author.

For permissions and inquiries, contact:
segunsong74@gmail.com

Cover design by Rena Song

Dedicated to Barbara Ferguson, whose enduring inspiration and guidance made this work possible

Table of Contents

AGENT ORANGE AND BIOPOLITICS

A Field of Discursive Silence

Introduction

While there is no national registry or an official number, the Vietnamese government estimates that there are more than 4.8 million Vietnamese people who are known to be exposed to the Agent Orange/dioxin sprayed during the Vietnam War and around 3 million Vietnamese have some form of health issues as a result[1]. Nearly 10 per cent of what was then South Vietnam was sprayed with the toxic chemical for nearly a decade from 1962 to 1971, causing serious health issues, including congenital disabilities and long-term neurological conditions, as well as extensive environmental damage (Martin, 2012).

Despite the large number of victims and the long-lasting effects of war on Vietnamese lives, the issue of Agent Orange is often described as

[1] The accurate number of Agent Orange victims is highly contested. 3 million is the number presented by the Vietnamese Association for Victims of Agent Orange (VAVA). The Vietnamese government endorses this figure.

"forgotten" in the West (Cooper, 2016; Nguyen & Hughes, 2017; Nguyen, 2021) and appears to hold limited salience in Vietnam as well, although current public attitudes are difficult to gauge. Existing studies suggest that the issue does not feature prominently as an urgent social concern or in everyday discourse (Song, 2022), a tendency that may be associated with shifting priorities among Vietnamese people, particularly younger generations, for whom engagement with Western-oriented economic opportunities and education has become increasingly important (Blattenberger, 2016).

Dioxin is widely regarded as one of the most toxic substances ever produced, however, establishing a direct causal relationship between dioxin exposure and specific health outcomes remains contested with interpretations of existing scientific evidence often shaped by researchers' and individuals' political orientations and discursive positions.

The research question emerges from the author's observation of a stark disparity in discourses surrounding Agent Orange: on the one hand, there are claims that millions have been affected, and on the other, there are assertions that the problem is exaggerated or did not occur[2]. Despite this polarisation, a prevailing silence persists, even as victims continue to suffer from long-term and intergenerational effects. The wide variation in estimating the number of victims points both to the scale of the issue and to the persistent uncertainty

[2] The former US ambassador to Vietnam, Michael W. Marine, said in 2007 "honestly I cannot say whether I have seen an Agent Orange victim or not."

surrounding it. Yet it remains striking that a problem of such magnitude appears to have limited public visibility, both in Vietnam and in the United States, in the absence of any definitive or officially recognised causal relationship.

This silence contrasts with other countries with similar war experience or colonial histories such as South Korea where the issues such as comfort women[3] and war compensation are still actively debated in the public arena. The silence also contrasts the US veterans and their families who sought the truth about what Agent Orange might have done to their loved ones and articulated their own experiences as a powerful counter-narrative to the dominant political and scientific discourses (Martin, 2012). This asymmetry aligns with broader critiques arguing that societies in the Global South have been systematically underrepresented in scholarship on the long-term health effects of war and trauma (Korinek et al., 2012).

As Palmer (2007) noted, current Agent Orange discussion is based on a simple inference that the issue has been largely forgotten. However, the effects of Agent Orange are ongoing and bound to resurface as there are many Vietnamese Agent Orange victims who are now second, third and even fourth generations[4] since the war. It is urgent

---

[3] The term "comfort women" refers to women and girls subjected to sexual slavery by the Japanese imperial military during the Asia–Pacific War, an issue that continues to be publicly debated and politically contested in South Korea and internationally (see Soh, 2008; Hayashi, 2015).

[4] VAVA estimates that approximately 150,000 second-generation victims, 35,000 third-generation victims, and around 2,000 fourth-generation victims are living in Vietnam today (Agent Orange Record, 2014).

that the potential multi-generational genetic effects of Agent Orange be addressed and contained. At the same time, many affected individuals have never experienced the war themselves, making the link between the war and their present condition difficult to understand, a situation that often results in psychological distress for victims who struggle to make sense of their disability and its consequences in everyday life.

This research examines key factors that contribute to the current silence surrounding Agent Orange, focusing on the ways scientific knowledge, political and diplomatic considerations, moral framing, and broader social and cultural conditions in contemporary Vietnam shape dominant discourse. This paper does not aim to interpret legal responsibility or make moral judgements, nor does it seek to propose solutions. Rather, it seeks to examine the extent of alienation between dominant discourse and the people to whom these discourses are meant to matter most, and to explore what underlies this gap.

This paper is organised as follows. It first outlines the theoretical foundations used to understand the Agent Orange issue and the complexities surrounding it. This section draws on existing literature on biopolitics, ideology, and the role of narrative in shaping both historical discourse and the lived experiences of victims. The paper then situates these theoretical frameworks within the postwar Vietnamese context, examining Đổi Mới, the economic reform, as a key marker in shaping contemporary Vietnam. This is followed by an analysis of how processes of economic development have created conditions under which biopolitical forms of governance have become prominent.

The paper then identifies four key mechanisms through which Vietnamese Agent Orange victims are discursively marginalised: (1) the use of scientific justification, (2) moral and political reframing, (3) selective representation, and (4) the erasure of victim agency. Drawing on the frameworks of biopolitics, ideology, and narrative identity, the paper shows how these mechanisms converge to produce a dominant discourse that is largely alienated from the lived realities of victims. This is followed by a critical discourse analysis based on victims' own voices, drawn from a range of Agent Orange literature and presented through first-person quotations. The analysis is informed by the author's long-term residence in Vietnam, which provided direct exposure to local discussions and everyday understandings of Agent Orange. These quotations reflect how Vietnamese Agent Orange victims understand the issue themselves, including how their disabilities and everyday lives have been shaped by it. The dataset highlights how victims are rendered silent subjects, stripped of political voice, symbolic recognition, and narrative authorship within a system structured by sovereign impunity and neoliberal developmentalism. At the end of the paper, it is suggested that alternative approaches can be imagined not as a "solution" to the Agent Orange issue, but as a humble reminder of human experience, through which a different course of action may be willed when a fuller understanding of human needs and social responsibility is revealed.

Theoretical Foundations

The main critical analysis of the paper draws on theories of biopolitics, ideology, and narrative identity. It situates these frameworks within postwar Vietnam, examining the impact of economic reforms such as Đổi Mới and how these reforms have provided conditions for biopolitical strategies to emerge. Four mechanisms through which Agent Orange victims are marginalised are identified: the use of scientific justification, moral and political reframing, selective representation, and the denial of agency. Viewed through the lenses of biopolitics, ideology, and narrative identity, these mechanisms reveal how victims are rendered silent subjects, stripped of recognition and their own voices within a system shaped by sovereign impunity and neoliberal development. These theoretical frameworks are introduced here as guiding analytical tools rather than as fully developed arguments. The Agent Orange issue is not an isolated occurrence but one embedded in broader social, political, and ideological structures, which require theoretical interpretation. Each framework will be further elaborated and applied in conjunction with the empirical analysis in later sections.

Biopolitics

This research employs biopolitics as a key analytical framework to address the central question of why a persistent silence surrounds the Agent Orange issue. Through this lens, the study examines both historical and contemporary developments, conceptualising Agent Orange as a biopolitical formation in which individual bodies become sites of political power and domination. In this sense, biopolitics serves as an analytical tool for understanding how Vietnamese victims and their conditions are governed and shaped by both domestic and international political forces.

The term biopolitics is not used as frequently in everyday political discourse as concepts such as party politics or identity politics. The biological meaning suggested by the prefix "bio[5]", unlike in terms such as biomedicine or biodiversity, does not provide an immediately discernible association when combined with politics. In philosophy and political thought, thinkers such as Schopenhauer, Nietzsche, Bergson, and Arendt [6] have reflected on life through different interpretations of *bios*, often grouped under the less widely known tradition of the philosophy of life (*Lebensphilosophie*) as discussed by

---

[5] *Bios*, meaning "life" in Latin language.

[6] Hannah Arendt (1958) had introduced the biological life as a political subject twenty years prior to Foucault through her idea of homo laborans in the human condition.

Lemke (2011). The first political scientist to use the term biopolitics was the Swedish scholar Rudolf Kjellén, who viewed the state as an organic entity in which different social groups struggle to articulate their interests (Lemke, 2011). However, it was not until the work of Michel Foucault in the 1970s that biopolitics gained wider recognition as a distinct concept in political philosophy.

Understanding the term *bios* in relation to the human body suggests that political processes are inevitably connected to biological life, as all political subjects have bodies which are carriers of life. However, the key to understanding biopolitics lies in examining the extent of the links between biological determinants and power within political processes. In this sense, the word biopolitics contains an apparent oxymoron. Politics has traditionally been understood as an attempt to transcend the necessities and limitations of bodily experience in order to establish social and collective relations (Lemke, 2011). By contrast, biopolitics insists that the body remains central to politics and cannot be separated from it.

In discussing biopolitics, it is first necessary to clarify where a given perspective is positioned along its conceptual spectrum. Differences in how the relationship between biological determinants and power is understood reflect an underlying tension between life as a biological condition and life as a subject of political control. At one end of this spectrum, where the link between biology and politics is understood as the most direct, political scientists focus on biological factors and their implications for political life. Drawing on theories and data from the life sciences, such as evolutionary biology and ethology, this approach seeks to explain human political behaviour through biological explanations (Somit & Peterson, 1998). Over time, this body of work was more broadly redefined as scientific biopolitics (Liesen & Walsh, 2012). From this perspective, life serves as the basis of politics, in the sense that biological processes are taken to account for political behaviour (Lemke, 2011). Contemporary examples include the regulation of human sexuality, homosexuality, reproductive policies, mortality and morbidity rates, as well as AIDS and disease control.

While these approaches establish the broader conceptual range of biopolitics, this research adopts a Foucauldian perspective, focusing on how power operates through the management of life rather than its biological explanation. In the context of Agent Orange, this enables an analysis of how victims' bodies are governed, classified, and rendered visible or invisible within institutional and political frameworks. This perspective is further extended through the works of Agamben and Hardt and Negri, and will be developed alongside the empirical analysis in subsequent sections.

Ideology, Fantasy, and Symbolic Apparatus

This section examines the role of ideology in enabling biopolitical governance in the context of Agent Orange, focusing on how dominant frameworks of meaning shape what can be said, recognised, or rendered silent in relation to victims' suffering. Ideology operates not only as a system of belief but as a practical mechanism through which affected populations are governed, norms are stabilised, and political responsibility is displaced. In this sense, ideology provides the symbolic and discursive conditions under which the marginalisation of Agent Orange victims is sustained and rendered natural.

In the Vietnamese context, official ideology rooted in Marxism–Leninism, reinforced through state-controlled education and media, plays a central role in shaping public understanding of Agent Orange. Despite significant economic transformation since the Communist takeover in 1975, socialist ideology remains institutionally embedded, providing an authoritative framework through which public discourse is organised and regulated. Drawing on Althusser's concept of ideology as an imaginary relation to real conditions of existence, and Lacan's notion of fantasy and *object petit a*, this section examines how state narratives manage contradictions, defer responsibility, and sustain political order, thereby contributing to the discursive marginalisation of Agent Orange victims. The symbolic apparatus, institutions, language, and norms produce and regulate meaning in society.

According to Althusser (1971), ideology is an imaginary representation of individuals' relation to their real conditions of existence. In other words, ideology refers to a way of relating to reality that does not directly correspond to material conditions. While classical Marxism assumes a relatively direct relationship between class position and lived conditions, Althusser offers a revised account in which social life is shaped by multiple determinations beyond economic relations alone. Contrary to Marx's expectation of intensifying class struggle, people often accept low wages and the system persists because although they remain proletarian, individuals inhabit diverse social roles, form families, pursue leisure, and orient themselves toward different aspirations. Ideology operates across these multiple sites, organising how social reality is perceived and lived. The various institutions and organisations comprising ideological state apparatuses form a system through which ideological formations are realised (p. 81). This insight constitutes Althusser's major contribution, while also marking a significant departure from classical Marxist assumptions. However, a key question arising here is how individuals become subjects of such practices, and what the precise mechanism is.

This account of what compels subjects to submit to authority points to dimensions of subjectivity irreducible to material determination, opening onto Freudian and Lacanian psychoanalysis, increasingly applied to analyses of late capitalism by theorists such as Slavoj Žižek. In Žižek's reformulation, ideology operates not only at the level of belief or representation but acquires an ontological dimension, structuring subjectivity prior to conscious reflection (1989). In order to grasp how ideology operates on individuals under modern capitalist social formations, it is therefore useful to understand Lacan's concept of *objet petit a* and the paradoxical relationship between content and form in ideology.

This conceptual framework will be further developed in the analysis section, where the interplay between ideology, fantasy, and symbolic structures is examined in relation to the lived experiences and discursive marginalisation of Agent Orange victims.

Narrative Identity and Temporality

This section shifts the focus to the lived experiences of Agent Orange victims, examining how their suffering is represented and understood within public discourse. It explores how dominant narratives shape what can be recognised, expressed, or silenced, and how victims' experiences often fail to align with these frameworks.

To analyse this, the section draws on the relationship between narrative and symbolic structures, where narrative organises meaning over time and symbolic systems define what can be said and recognised. In Foucauldian terms, narratives actively produce regimes of truth, determining who can speak and with what authority.

Søren Kierkegaard famously held that life must be understood backwards but lived forwards, an insight grounded in his awareness of human finitude. This claim resonates with Martin Heidegger's later account of non-linear temporality, although Kierkegaard did not develop it as a systematic theory of time. Within this existential framework, individuals confront the consequences of their choices across a lifetime, a process Kierkegaard understood as the pursuit of truth. Crucially, this process is not linear but temporally layered: past experiences and future possibilities continuously shape the present. The self thus emerges through the dynamic interplay between memory of the past, anticipation of the future, and decisions enacted in the present (Kierkegaard, 1980).

Paul Ricoeur (1984), best known for his hermeneutics of selfhood, paid close attention to the temporality of human existence and the nature of instantaneity. He redefined human existence in terms of a definitive and essential temporal structure. For Ricoeur, the only way to make sense of the impermanence of finite being is through narration, by recounting events and actions that disrupt the prevailing order and reorganize it. This process, which he referred to as *auto-positioning* (Stanford, 2025), enables the creation of new meaning beyond what currently stands, through which forgiveness and reconciliation may become possible.

This dynamic is best explained through his theory of narrative identity, which involves the dialectic between *idem* and *ipse* identities. *Idem* identity is rooted in sameness, what remains consistent over time, whereas *ipse* identity refers to selfhood, the evolving aspect of being. The presence of *ipse* identity suggests that the self is better understood through the question "Who am I?", a self defined through lived history, relationships, and responsibility, rather than "What am I?", which points to fixed attributes or categories (Ricoeur, 1992).

Martin Heidegger pursued the question of Being through a phenomenological investigation of how human existence is shaped by time. Like Kierkegaard and Ricoeur, Heidegger rejected the idea of being as something fixed or timeless. Instead, he argued that being is always situated in history, unfolding within time and fundamentally shaped by it (1962). Time, for Heidegger, is therefore not a background given passively but the basic condition through which Being becomes intelligible.

For Heidegger, time is not merely a sequence of measurable moments or a linear progression of discrete "nows." He instead offers an existential account of temporality as a unified structure composed of three interrelated dimensions: the retention of the past, the anticipation of the future, and engagement with the present. These are not successive stages but elements of a continuous, interwoven experience, which Heidegger terms *ecstatic temporality* (1982). Human existence stretches beyond the present moment, as the past persists as heritage and the future appears as possibility. Temporality thus functions as a horizon of understanding, enabling meaning to emerge through the relation between the no-longer, the not-yet, and the now. From this perspective, the common conception of time as a mere succession of isolated points fails to grasp its fundamental role in making understanding possible, a view Heidegger explicitly criticizes as "a manifold and succession of nows" (1982, p. 123).

Taken together, these perspectives suggest that human experience is not simply lived in time but is organised through narrative structures that give coherence to suffering, memory, and identity. In the context of Agent Orange, this framework provides a way of approaching how victims' experiences may be shaped not only by material conditions but also by the temporal and narrative forms through which they are interpreted and represented. These conceptual tools will be developed further in the analysis section, where their relevance will be examined in relation to victims' testimonies and broader discursive practices.

Đổi Mới (renovation), development and biopolitics in Vietnam

Building on the bodies of literature examined above, the following section analyses the biopolitical conditions of contemporary Vietnam, focusing on how biopolitical governance has operated upon the population through the country's socio-economic and political development. This discussion provides the groundwork for a subsequent analysis of how the Agent Orange issue is positioned within, and shaped by, Vietnam's intersecting political and developmental agendas.

The economic reforms of Đổi Mới, initiated in 1986, radically transformed Vietnam's economy and social order, shifting the country from prolonged poverty under centralized rule toward market-oriented growth, and national development. This transition provided a new source of legitimacy for one-party rule for the Vietnamese Communist Party, allowing it to frame poverty in relation to individual affairs rather than a structural condition. As in other neoliberalising economies, social welfare provision declined and was replaced by market-driven policies that prioritise productivity over vulnerability, particularly affecting people with disabilities and those considered less economically productive. While the economic gains of the past three decades have been significant, this developmental success has also reoriented public attention toward the future rather than the past (Small, 2021). Yet the escape from poverty that underpins Vietnam's developmental trajectory continues to shape the material and ideological realities of everyday life, furnishing the state with key modalities of biopolitical governance (Gupta, 2012).

Within this growth-oriented paradigm, economic growth becomes an unquestioned imperative that legitimises sacrifice in the name of progress. Those unable to contribute economically, including people with disabilities and Agent Orange victims, are rendered marginal to national concern, their needs subordinated to the pursuit of prosperity. The interplay of neoliberal and socialist rationalities thus produces a system in which success is celebrated, failure is stigmatised, and the suffering of the most vulnerable is systematically obscured.

Đổi Mới (renovation)

As neo-Marxists, Negri and Hardt (2000) argue that the conditions of production within a globalised biopolitical machine are in constant flux, and these conditions offer a useful analytical angle for understanding contemporary society. In the Vietnamese context, grasping the significance of Đổi Mới, its scale, nature, and implications, is essential to understanding these broader processes of transformation.

The Communist Party of Vietnam initiated Đổi Mới at its Sixth National Congress in 1986, marking a shift toward a market-oriented economy characterised by the recognition of private ownership, the promotion of entrepreneurship, the de-collectivisation of landholdings, the decentralisation of economic planning, increased consumer production, and the expansion of trade and foreign investment relations (Communist Party of Vietnam, 1987).

Despite prevailing confidence and optimism within the North Vietnamese government following its military victory in the mid-

1970s, Vietnam's economy stagnated after reunification in 1976 due to multiple factors, including declining aid from the Soviet Union, the suspension of international assistance following the invasion of Cambodia, harsh climatic conditions, widespread infrastructure destruction, persistent trade deficits, and high inflation. Following the withdrawal of US forces from South Vietnam, the subsidiary economy that had been sustained beyond its inherent productive capacity by the presence of American troops, through mechanisms such as the Commercial Import Program (CIP) and direct US military expenditures in local currency, collapsed altogether (Marr & White, 1988).

As economic stagnation deepened, internal recognition of systemic failure began to surface within the Party leadership. The incoming Secretary-General Truong Chinh, a key supporter of the adoption of Đổi Mới, openly acknowledged the malfunctioning of the economy, stating:

We have made mistakes due to "leftist infantilism," idealism, and the contravention of the objective laws of socio-economic development. These mistakes were manifested in the emphasis on developing heavy industry on a large scale beyond our practical capacity and in maintaining a bureaucratically centralised mechanism of economic management based on state subsidies, supported by an oversized superstructure that overburdened the infrastructure. As a result, we relied largely on foreign aid for our subsistence (Communist Party of Vietnam, 1986, p. 25).

The government acknowledged that responsibility for the economic downturn no longer lay with colonialism, imperialism, or war, but with the failure of an economic policy that had prioritised a heavy-industry-oriented development model, partly inspired by South Korea (Marr & White, 1988). The official adoption of Đổi Mới was, in fact, grounded in nearly a decade of famine and in the widespread reliance on informal and illegal commercial activities that people undertook to compensate for severe food shortages, practices that the state tacitly tolerated (Ebbighausen, 2015). More significantly, momentum toward reform emerged from the success of farming cooperatives, which reorganised collective labour into quasi-social enterprises by distributing surplus production beyond state quotas to their members.

Vietnam has experienced remarkable economic growth since the implementation of Đổi Mới. The private sector expanded at an extraordinary pace, with the contribution of the non-state sector to the state budget rising from 51 billion VND in 1991 to 7,405 billion VND in 2001, representing a 145-fold increase within a decade (Vo Van That & Hoang Xuan Son, 2023). By 2024, GDP per capita had reached USD $4,624, more than ten times the level recorded in 1986 (USD $430). Over the same period, Vietnam's poverty rate fell dramatically, with the poverty headcount at national poverty lines at around 4.2 percent in 2022 from around 75 per cent before Đổi Mới (World Bank, 2023), illustrating how sustained growth has translated into widespread improvements in living standards.

Đổi Mới not only lifted millions out of poverty but fundamentally restructured Vietnam's conditions of production. Market reforms dismantled the centrally planned allocation system and reintroduced private ownership, household-based production, and foreign investment as central economic mechanisms. In doing so, the reform shifted the organisation of labour and surplus extraction from state redistribution to market coordination, embedding Vietnam within global supply chains. This transformation diverged from the classical Marxist vision of proletarian emancipation. Rather, it generated a new capitalist configuration in which low wages, labour discipline, and political stability functioned as structural advantages within global markets. The material improvements that followed were not merely rhetorical claims but visible changes in everyday life, reinforcing the perception that continued integration into the global economy was both necessary and beneficial.

The apparent success of the policy changed the everyday life of Vietnamese people and nationwide living standards dramatically. Amid these rapid changes, the priority of the political system in Vietnam is and has always been about maintaining the power of the Vietnamese Communist Party and state apparatus (Hayton, 2010). Historically, resistance to foreign domination, national independence, and reunification provided the political legitimacy for one-party rule. In the post-reunification and post-market reform era, however, this basis of legitimacy has shifted. The survival of the Communist Party increasingly depends on performance, particularly the delivery of economic growth, material prosperity, and improved living standards which had been long denied to the population. Enabled by the capitalist market through Đổi Mới, the household re-emerged as the primary economic unit and a renewed site of political intervention and governance. This broad acceptance of global economic integration and market rationality has, in turn, created favourable conditions for the state to overtly pursue its biopolitical agenda. This agenda operates within a broader logic of growth and market integration, in which social value becomes increasingly tied to productivity and economic participation, while forms of life that fall outside these criteria are rendered marginal.

Developmentalism as a ruling ideology

The widespread poverty experienced during and after Vietnam's prolonged wars gave way to a nationwide postwar development drive following the success of Đổi Mới. However, the uncritical endorsement of economic development by both domestic and international actors elevated development to the status of an uncontested ideology, effectively granting it political authority that leaves little space for resistance (Bekkevold et al., 2021). In this context, the post-reform period saw "development" (phát triển) emerge as a key term that not only shaped the dominant ideology sustaining the socialist state's mode of governance but also reoriented the aspirations of an increasingly ambitious population, thereby providing a central modality for biopolitical control. As Vietnam integrated into the global economy, market mechanisms and neoliberal rationalities, productivity, target attainment, and the figure of the "self-enterprising" individual became operational as both practical instruments and philosophical foundations of the prevailing development orientation.

These capitalist discourses are often obscured by a nationalist ethos, in which national independence and poverty reduction are presented as collective achievements. Within this framework, the symbolic apparatus, comprising education, media, official slogans, and policy rhetoric, frames economic inequality through narratives of personal failure, recasting structural disadvantage as moral deficiency within the developmentalist ethos.

However, these changes pose direct challenges to the conventional values of socialist ideology. In short, neoliberal, individualistic ideals are at odds with the egalitarian principles hitherto upheld by socialist regimes as core communist values. For example, welfare provision, as a means of achieving equality, had been central to the socialist ideal; however, integration into the global economic order, led by major global financial institutions, compelled a shift from universal welfare provision under a centralised planning system to targeted assistance (Kandiyoti, 1999). This policy reorientation toward "socialisation" (xã hội hóa), which counterintuitively denotes the transfer of responsibility from the state to individuals and families, followed (Nguyen, 2018). In the 1990s, Vietnam's annual spending on social welfare accounted for approximately 4–8 per cent of national GDP, but this figure fell to around 1 per cent by 2015 (World Bank, 2005). Vietnam's public spending on social assistance has since remained significantly lower than that of other developing Asian countries (Leung, 2024). This shift has adversely affected those who now fall outside official definitions of poverty, supporting Harriss's (2007) argument that Vietnam's poverty reduction statistics are partly illusory, shaped by definitional and measurement practices that fail to accurately identify affected populations.

By and large, the Vietnamese Communist Party's policy over the past three decades can be understood as a response to this reality. The Party has navigated this path with considerable success while continuing to uphold growth-driven ideologies that mobilise the labour force and, at the same time, discipline and subordinate the population. The adverse effects of neoliberal development on individuals are not openly acknowledged under the continued invocation of socialist principles. Yet the Vietnamese government retains the capacity to criticise neoliberal development models by appealing to a socialist notion of equity (*công bằng xã hội*), in which national economic growth is framed as the means through which social equity and socialist goals will ultimately be achieved (London, 2014).

For instance, the Poverty Reduction and Growth Strategy, a key government policy document on poverty eradication, cites former President Hồ Chí Minh's declaration that poverty is an enemy of the nation and that it is the nation's mission to overcome it in order to attain a prosperous and happy life (Socialist Republic of Vietnam, 2002). By appealing to the authority of the nation's founding father, individuals are encouraged to become agents of national development, with participation framed as a source of moral worth and personal dignity. Under earlier communist ideals, poverty was collectively shared and imbued with pride, particularly in representations of the proletariat and peasantry. Lương (2003) notes a period of temporary acceptance of shared poverty, alongside an emphasis on relative equality across rural and urban communities. Although limited in scope, the state exercised redistributive power and provided support to the poor during the subsidy period of 1975–1986, largely sustained by Soviet aid. Even within this framework, however, social hierarchies persisted, with greater entitlements accorded to Party members, state officials, and the families of war veterans (Kerkvliet, 2011).

However, within the reconfigured ideological landscape, state discourse has been reframed to reconcile market-oriented development with socialist moral claims. The socialist government now promotes slogans such as "Wealthy Citizens, Strong Nation" (*Dân giàu, nước mạnh*) (Bayly, 2013), aligning the development ethos with moral virtue. The term "class" has largely disappeared from official discourse and has been replaced with "socio-economic difference," while the adverse effects of neoliberal realities, such as growing inequality, remain unrecognised and are instead attributed to individual failure and innate deficiencies (Lincoln, 2023). Poverty is now depicted as a deficit of particular social groups whose supposedly unimprovable qualities prevent them from participating in and benefiting from national economic growth (MacLean, 2013).

Such a paradigm shift legitimises the reduction of welfare provision while the governing rationality grounded in socialist ideology remains intact. Meanwhile, Vietnam's economic performance continues to provide its communist government with an external governing rationality and a form of indemnity against criticism, as it has been widely lauded for its success in poverty reduction and presented as an exemplary case by international NGOs and aid organisations, often while overlooking the significant increase in inequality within the socialist country. In 2009, according to available statistics, the poorest quintile received 6.6 per cent of social benefits, while the top quintile received almost 40 per cent (Gao, Evans, & Garfinkel, 2012). The capitalist-oriented market, which promises more affluent lifestyles as a pathway out of poverty, is unlikely to be identified as a source of social problems in post-reform Vietnam, where many compare present conditions only with past extreme poverty and therefore fully embrace and celebrate the capitalist system (Bayly, 2013).

While the capitalist system, featuring new discourses of individuality, freedom, and choice, is now embraced and celebrated, contemporary Vietnam continues to witness significant sacrifices in human labour, the environment, cultural traditions, and social bonds, all made in the name of development. These sacrifices are legitimised within the prevailing narrative of rapid economic growth, underpinned by the conviction that development will fulfil the population's capitalist aspirations, generate new opportunities, and secure material abundance long denied by decades of hardship (Hayton, 2010; Salemink, 2019). As Tan (2011) points out, this strategy of deploying the language of empowerment can mute discourses of resistance by operationalising contestable notions of participation, ownership, partnership, poverty reduction, and development, thereby disabling emancipatory politics. For example, Vietnam's contemporary formal education system emphasises the production of competent young achievers capable of meeting the demands of economic niches in a globalised world, and the pursuit of entry into this space facilitates both the production and subjugation of docile bodies indifferent to the disjuncture between neo-liberal realities and the rhetoric of socialist ideals (Bayly, 2013). This process reinforces the notion that bodies deemed unproductive within the development project constitute a burden on families and communities.

It is against this ideological backdrop that the issue of Agent Orange has evolved within Vietnam's domestic policy domain and shaped the state's approach to its management and representation.

Biopolitics in Vietnam

Biopolitics and the Governance of Population in Vietnam

This section of the literature demonstrates how biopolitics operates in Vietnam. It functions primarily at the level of populations through the regulation of individual biological bodies. Here, the biological body becomes central to processes of subjugation while simultaneously generating broader effects of population management, in line with Foucault's conception of biopolitical governance.

The concept of "population quality" occupies a central place in Vietnamese policy discourse, through which the state asserts authority to enhance, manage, and regulate the population in the name of national development. This policy reflects the convergence of historical and cultural legacies with Vietnam's neoliberal ideological positioning. Within this framework, biopolitical rationality is enacted through policies and practices that govern reproduction, productivity, and social value, shaping who is rendered productive, supported, or excluded.

Importantly, this form of biopolitics is not oriented toward the maximisation of life per se, but toward the extraction of maximum utility from bodies in the service of development (Weheliye, 2014). Under this logic, the body becomes a basic economic unit of production, while forms of debility or barriers to productive labour are framed as obstacles to national progress and are selectively managed or eliminated (Puar, 2017).

This biopolitical orientation is further sustained by deeply embedded cultural and ideological traditions. Paternalistic state authority remains intertwined with norms of collectivism, group orientation, and filial obligation, shaped by the politico-religious legacies of Confucianism, Daoism, and Buddhism (Salemink & Nguyen, 2019). These traditions lend moral legitimacy to state intervention in intimate domains of life, framing governance not as coercion but as paternal guardianship. Within this normative framework, social value is defined relationally and collectively, privileging contribution, sacrifice, and endurance over individual rights. Reproductive and life-course decisions are thus shaped through internalised norms of responsibility and obligation to an imagined national family.

"Population quality" as a governing rationality

The notion of "population quality" (chất lượng dân số) is frequently invoked in Vietnamese policy discourse and bears resemblance to China's suzhi[7] (素質) framework. Importantly, it does not correspond directly to the Western concept of "quality of life," which would more accurately be translated as chất lượng cuộc sống[8]. Instead, population quality refers to the perceived biological, moral, and productive attributes of the population itself.

An official policy statement illustrates this logic clearly:

"to reduce morbidity and mortality, promote health and increase life expectancy, improve the quality of our race (nâng cao chất lượng dân số) and contribute to improving the quality of life ... in response to the needs of industrialization, modernization, nation-building and defence" (Communist Party of Vietnam, 2005)

This statement contains a clear normative judgement: in order to sustain economic development, the quality of the population must be actively managed and improved. Within this biopolitical view, bodies are rendered as instruments of development, and state intervention into reproduction, health, and education becomes necessary.

This biopolitical rationality is operationalised through a range of institutional mechanisms that extend beyond reproductive policy and

---

[7] Translated generally as quality of life or human quality.

[8] In Vietnamese policy discourse, chất lượng dân số differs fundamentally from chất lượng cuộc sống ("quality of life"). While the latter concerns individual welfare and living conditions, population quality refers to the biological, moral, and productive attributes of the population as a collective target of state intervention.

into the formation of subjects themselves. Formal education plays a key role within this governing rationality, functioning not only as a site of skill formation but as a mechanism of population management. As Bayly (2013) argues, education in Vietnam operates as a disciplinary apparatus within the broader symbolic order, shaping aspirations through the emotional and moral coding of success, productivity, and patriotic contribution. It combines the propaganda of the old socialist ideological order with the regimes of endless competition characteristic of capitalism, aligning individual desires with state-driven narratives of development and national progress, while regulating population quality through differentiated access to opportunity, status, and mobility.

Biopolitical techniques: reproduction and bureaucratic classification

Family planning and reproductive regulation

Gammeltoft (2014) argues that an ethnographically grounded analysis is essential for understanding how biopolitics operates in Vietnam, showing how neoliberal rationalities are mediated, and rendered culturally intelligible through historically embedded moral and social frameworks. Drawing on field research, she demonstrates that reproductive regulation functions as a central mechanism through which the state manages population quality. Reproductive decision-making is framed in the name of poverty eradication and national development, with the regulation of sexuality operating as a means of imposing communal values rooted in collective responsibility and moral obligation.[9]

Family planning has constituted a key site of Vietnamese biopolitics since the early 1960s, when it was initially introduced in response to rapid population growth and perceived food shortages (Jones, 1982). Although abortion services were suspended during the war period (Zeigler, 1996), population pressures following national reunification prompted renewed state intervention. Contraception and abortion were subsequently formalised within childbearing policies and expanded significantly in scope and institutional reach during the post-Đổi Mới period (Goodkind, 1994; Gammeltoft, 2014). Over time, reproductive governance increasingly extended into private health sectors, further normalising intervention into intimate reproductive decisions (Turley & Selden, 1993).

Recent statistics indicate that Vietnam continues to exhibit one of the highest abortion ratios globally, with approximately 68 abortions per 1,000 live births reported in 2020–2021, one of the highest rates in Asia (UNFPA Vietnam, 2022). This pattern has remained relatively stable for over three decades. Rather than reflecting individualised choice alone, reproductive decisions are shaped by broader social

[9] Gammeltoft situates these communal values within long-standing narratives of shared ancestry and biological continuity in Vietnam. She notes the enduring symbolic force of the folktale of Lạc Long Quân and Âu Cơ, in which a dragon father and mountain fairy mother produce one hundred eggs that hatch into the ancestors of the Vietnamese people. This myth of common origin has historically underpinned notions of national unity and biological cohesion and has been repeatedly mobilised in nationalist discourse, including by President Hồ Chí Minh, as a source of endurance and collective responsibility (Gammeltoft, 2014, p. 64).

pressures surrounding productivity, family responsibility, and the anticipated social and economic burden of disability. Abortion thus operates within a biopolitical logic that links reproductive outcomes to collective futures and population-level optimisation, with interventions disproportionately concentrated among married women in their peak childbearing years (Goodkind, 1994; UNFPA Vietnam, 2022).

Bureaucratic classification: lý lịch

Alongside reproductive regulation, another key mechanism of biopolitical control in Vietnam is the *lý lịch* (personal biography), which, like disability certification, classifies individuals and fixes their social position within hierarchies of political loyalty, productivity, and social value. Similar to practices historically employed in China, the Vietnamese Communist Party has used *lý lịch* dossiers to categorise subjects according to family background, wartime affiliation, ethnicity, occupation, and religion. Following national reunification, this system functioned explicitly as a tool of political differentiation, enabling the state to identify ideological allegiance and apply discriminatory policies accordingly (Goscha, 2017, p. 417). These policies restricted access to education and public-sector employment for the children of those deemed politically suspect, while rewarding the descendants of North Vietnamese soldiers and revolutionary families recognised for their sacrifice to the nation (Goscha, 2017, p. 418). For example, differential cut-off scores were applied in civil service and academic recruitment examinations based on ideological classification, region, and ethnicity.

Although the overtly punitive function of *lý lịch* has formally diminished, the practice itself persists. Every adult Vietnamese citizen is still required to submit a personal biography, and similar documentation is now widely used across both public and private sectors. In this respect, *lý lịch* increasingly resembles employment screening practices found elsewhere, such as autobiographical statements in South Korea or curricula vitae in Western contexts. Viewed in this light, the *lý lịch* system exemplifies a broader biopolitical logic in Vietnam. Like disability certification and family planning policies, it operates as a classificatory technology that categorises, ranks, and excludes individuals according to perceived value, loyalty, and social worth, thereby shaping access to education, employment, and state support. Following Foucault's broader conception of biopolitics as the governance of life at the level of populations rather than the management of biological bodies alone, *lý lịch* can be understood as a biopolitical device insofar as it regulates life chances and social legitimacy, even in the absence of direct reference to individual biological attributes.

Agent Orange as symbolic and affective biopolitical governance

Within this broader biopolitical framework, the issue of Agent Orange has been mobilised as a powerful symbolic apparatus. According to Gammeltoft (2014), graphic images of bodily deformation in newborns and narratives of parental suffering rendered Vietnamese society more receptive to state reproductive policies. Such emotionally charged reactions were taken up by the government as part of its biopolitical interventions.

This symbolic management extends beyond reproductive control into the realm of social visibility. Vietnam persistently operates within a forward-looking developmental mode, in which "development" functions as a dominant signifier legitimising a wide range of state practices and reinforcing national unity. Those who fall outside this trajectory are readily marked as unworthy members of society and subjected to stigma and exclusion.

This logic becomes particularly visible in the Vietnam Association for Victims of Agent Orange (VAVA)'s community engagement strategies. The promotion of "shining examples" showcases Agent Orange victims who demonstrate social contribution (Hopton & Walton, 2018). This strategy seeks to reassure the public that these individuals are not a burden and do not impede national progress. Notably, this approach aligns closely with Confucian traditions prioritising collectivism and contribution over individual rights. Within this logic, recognition and inclusion are conditional, based upon productivity.

VAVA's use of awards, media representation, and exemplary narratives illustrates how inclusion and exclusion are mobilised as key techniques of biopolitical governance. It is within this framework that the logic of conditional inclusion is strictly applied to Agent Orange victims.

Methodology

The research is informed by ethnographic experience and adopts a critical-constructivist paradigm, utilising qualitative methods and critical discourse analysis. By comparing victims' narratives with state and institutional discourses, the study exposes asymmetries in representation and recognition. Purposive sampling and thematic coding allow for a structured comparison of how meaning, responsibility, and memory are constructed across domains of power. The analysis is further informed by Vietnamese-language sources, which introduce locally mediated narratives that are underrepresented in English-language scholarship.

Researcher Positionality

Over a period of more than five years in Vietnam, the author worked across multiple roles for international aid organisations, including as a staff member, consultant, and volunteer, and also served as a university lecturer in social work. One such organisation, funded by USAID, focused on disability services, including those for Agent Orange victims. Although these professional roles were not limited exclusively to Agent Orange–affected populations, such individuals were frequently encountered within broader disability-focused projects. Of particular relevance was the organisation's work on improving mobility and functional independence for people with disabilities, including Agent Orange victims, which enabled the development of early observations and a sustained research interest in the silence surrounding this large-scale humanitarian and political issue. This analytical focus was further informed by a targeted field trip undertaken specifically for Vietnamese-language data collection and contextual verification. Through these engagements, informal interviews were conducted with victims and interactions took place with a range of stakeholders, including VAVA officials, thereby laying the groundwork for the present inquiry.

Research Paradigm

This study adopts a critical-constructivist paradigm, drawing on ideas from critical theory as an interpretive frame rather than a prescriptive method. The aim is to understand how power, ideology, and political interests shape what is said and what is left unsaid about Agent Orange and its victims. Critical theory helps identify how victims' voices are excluded or spoken for, particularly in state and institutional narratives. This approach aligns with the use of Critical Discourse Analysis, which provides tools to examine both the structure and content of language across different texts and to demonstrate how meaning is shaped by context and relations of power.

This study also adopts a qualitative research approach, which is appropriate given that the research seeks to explore the meanings, perceptions, and representations embedded in language. Qualitative research is particularly suited to inquiries into how social phenomena are constructed and experienced, especially in contexts where voice, memory, and power are contested. As Denzin and Lincoln (2018) explain, qualitative research is concerned not with generalisation or measurement, but with understanding the processes and discourses through which people and institutions make sense of the world. In the case of Agent Orange, the central concern lies not only in what is articulated, but also in how it is expressed, by whom, and under what conditions or constraints. This approach allows for an in-depth analysis of narratives, silences, and framing devices that cannot be adequately captured through quantitative methods. The inclusion of Vietnamese-language materials further strengthens this approach by enabling analyses of locally embedded expressions of suffering and meaning that are not fully visible in English-language institutional sources.

To operationalise this framework, the analysis proceeds on two interrelated levels, designed to capture how Agent Orange is articulated differently across sites of power and lived experience. Purposive sampling is employed not to ensure representativeness, but to enable analytical comparison between dominant discursive forms and marginalised voices.

Discursive Form: State and Institutional Regimes of Meaning

This perspective examines how Agent Orange is framed within state, institutional, and expert discourses, focusing on scientific, geopolitical, humanitarian, and policy-oriented narratives. The analytical emphasis is on discourse as form, that is, on the symbolic and epistemic structures that organise meaning prior to particular statements. This includes dominant vocabularies, explanatory paradigms, and governing logics through which Agent Orange is rendered intelligible and governable within official and expert domains.

The material for this perspective draws from a combination of sources, including media observation, policy and scientific texts, institutional publications, and insights gained through engagement with victims and relevant stakeholders during ethnographic fieldwork in Vietnam. The analysis does not concentrate on the detailed content of individual narratives, but rather on how meaning is mediated through symbolic apparatuses that frame and regulate interpretation: which paradigms are privileged, which voices are authorised, and how authority is consolidated within institutional discourse. This approach foregrounds questions of epistemic justice, particularly the risk that victims' voices are appropriated, filtered, or reframed in ways that displace their intended meaning and subordinate them to institutional priorities.

Discursive Counter-Position: Victims' Lived Articulation

This perspective examines first-person testimonies and lived experiences of Agent Orange victims. The analysis focuses on discourse as content, attending to how victims articulate suffering, responsibility, and agency in their own words. These narratives are analysed in relation to state and institutional discourses, particularly where themes of political framing, selective visibility, and constrained agency recur. Rather than treating victim accounts in isolation, the study situates them within the institutionally mediated structures of meaning that shape recognition and interpretation.

The material for this perspective is drawn from a systematically and purposively assembled dataset of first-person narratives, primarily sourced from Vietnamese-language media and locally mediated accounts. The dataset preserves victims' direct quotations and aligns them with identified critical themes, providing the empirical foundation for examining how victims articulate their realities in contrast to dominant institutional framings.

Critical Discourse Analysis (CDA) dataset

The second perspective consists of a structured critical discourse analysis, drawing on a total of 100 sources (N=100). Of these, 50 (N=50) represent victims' discourse, defined strictly as texts containing direct quotations from Agent Orange victims, and 50 (N=50) represent Vietnamese state and institutional discourse, including state media, official statements, and policy documents.

Using an assisted thematic coding approach, both sets of discourses were analysed and compared across emergent thematic categories. The aim is to examine critically whether and how victims' voices are genuinely represented within broader political narratives. This approach illustrates how asymmetries in visibility and framing power constitute a symbolic apparatus in which some narratives are amplified while others are silenced, thereby producing epistemic injustice.

Taken together, this two-perspective critical discourse analysis reveals how the dynamics between form (the symbolic apparatus dominated by state and institutions) and content (victims' lived experience) fail to converge, producing the epistemic injustice that structures the contemporary understanding of the Agent Orange issue.

Spatially Situated Data Collection and Discursive Visibility

The secondary data collection conducted in Vietnam yielded outcomes that differed markedly from searches conducted in Australia where the author is based, even when materials were nominally available online. This divergence reflects not only linguistic differences, but also the political economy of information circulation and visibility. Vietnamese-language sources, particularly provincial media and locally hosted platforms, are more readily surfaced through domestic search environments, local indexing practices, and context-specific keyword conventions that do not translate directly into English queries.

In addition, algorithmic filtering, regional content prioritisation, and platform-specific access conditions mean that certain materials, while nominally public, are effectively obscured or deprioritised for users searching from outside Vietnam. Conducting secondary data collection in Vietnam therefore enabled access to a broader and more locally embedded corpus of materials, strengthening the empirical foundation of the study and allowing for a more balanced analysis of Agent Orange discourse across linguistic and institutional contexts.

Methodological Scope and Constraints

This study acknowledges several methodological constraints arising from its qualitative and purposive design. First, the dataset is not intended to be statistically representative but analytically focused, privileging depth, discursivity, and comparative insight over generalisation. The objective is not to measure prevalence but to illuminate structures of meaning and asymmetries of representation across discursive domains.

Second, a degree of linguistic asymmetry exists between English-language and Vietnamese-language materials. This does not concern the presence or absence of victim voices per se, but the discursive conditions under which those voices appear. While English-language sources include first-person testimonies, these accounts are more frequently embedded within institutional, humanitarian, or policy-oriented frameworks that shape how suffering is rendered legible. Vietnamese-language materials, by contrast, more often present direct expressions of everyday need, frustration, and loss, sometimes in pragmatic or minimally mediated forms. This divergence reflects differing regimes of representation rather than differences in lived experience.

Third, the use of translated Vietnamese materials entails an unavoidable risk of semantic compression or interpretive slippage. This is mitigated by retaining original quotations where possible and by directing analytical attention toward broader discursive patterns rather than fine-grained lexical nuances.

Given the constraints of length, it is not feasible to reproduce the full discursive context of each quotation included in the dataset. The excerpts are therefore treated not as isolated statements but as nodes within broader discursive formations. Selection was guided by recurring linguistic patterns, institutional registers, and narrative structures identified across complete source texts. In this sense, the analytical focus lies less in the individual sentence as a self-contained claim than in its function within a larger field of meaning production. All quotations were verified against their original context to ensure that they reflect dominant framing logics rather than exceptional or decontextualized remarks.

Taken together, these constraints delineate the scope of the study while remaining consistent with the epistemological commitments of critical discourse analysis, which foregrounds mediation, power, and exclusion as constitutive features of meaning-making rather than as threats to validity.

Characteristics of Agent Orange Discourse

This section identifies key characteristics of Agent Orange discourse as evidence of a structural discrepancy between dominant institutional narratives and subordinated victims' voices. Agent Orange constitutes an exceptionally complex issue, requiring knowledge across diverse domains, including politics, foreign relations, science, law, humanitarian assistance, and culture, reflecting the multiplicity of fields involved. Most existing discourses have developed within these respective domains, with science and health emerging as the most extensively researched perspectives. It is also notable that, although many studies draw on data collected from Vietnamese Agent Orange victims, relatively few place victims themselves at the centre of analysis.

The analytical categories presented here, scientific justification, moral reframing, selective representation, and lack of agency, are all symptoms of this structural discrepancy. Scientific discourse functions as a filter, muting Vietnamese victims by demanding scientific evidence and proof of causality. Political and moral discourse often positions the Vietnamese state as mediator or gatekeeper, framing the issue in ways that deflect internal responsibility while minimising any political risk the issue might pose to national unity and biopolitical control. Selective framing celebrates international partnerships and developmental milestones, providing the means through which the issue is signified within designated institutional domains. By contrast, victims are largely confined to narratives of suffering and passive victimhood. Institutional actors, meanwhile, occupy the visible symbolic space through which meaning is organised and political authority is reinforced.

Most striking among these characteristics is the lack of agency. In government discourse, victims rarely appear as subjects. They do not emerge as agents within the symbolic exchanges that frame suffering, life and war, and victimhood, particularly as these are attributed to American responsibility. Victims are not positioned as actors of movement, decision-making, or organised social action. Their presence is implied rather than voiced through recognised channels. The result is a discursive field in which victims' experiences do not intervene in or reshape official narratives but are instead absorbed and neutralised by a language and system of signifiers that prioritise order, normativity, and the preservation of the status quo. Taken together, these four characteristics reflect not only the complexity of the Agent Orange issue but also provide analytical dimensions through which the operation of the symbolic apparatus can be critically examined.

1. The use of scientific justification

One of the defining characteristics of the Agent Orange issue is that the legitimacy of its harmful effects has been overwhelmingly framed through scientific statements produced in the United States. This framing has simultaneously limited public understanding of the issue and functioned to indemnify US responsibility. The precise consequences of Agent Orange exposure for the Vietnamese population remain a site of intense scientific controversy, not because harm is unlikely, but because establishing definitive causal certainty is structurally difficult. Isolating the effects of Agent Orange from multiple, overlapping symptoms associated with illness is technically complex, if not impossible. Dioxin persists in the human body over long periods due to its chemical stability and its capacity to accumulate in fatty tissue, where it may remain dormant across generations (WHO, 2010). Its effects may skip a generation and reappear in the grandchildren of those exposed, further complicating epidemiological research (Hoang Ba Thinh, 2006). Meeting the rigid methodological standards demanded for scientific proof would require long-term laboratory testing on human subjects, a requirement frequently invoked to dismiss existing evidence. Critics have noted that laboratory-based methodologies, which isolate substances from lived conditions, systematically overlook factors such as poverty, limited healthcare access, environmental contamination, and chronic stress, all of which shape health outcomes in Agent Orange–affected communities (McHugh, 2011).

From a discursive perspective, scientific uncertainty does not merely describe the problem; it constitutes the problem itself. The controversy that follows is therefore not incidental but actively produced, sustained, and positioned as the primary site of contestation. Even if further evidence were to emerge, it would likely remain disputed, since assessments of scientific authority are often shaped by researchers' institutional affiliations, particularly their alignment with state agencies or victim communities[10] (McCulloch, 1984). Scientific disagreement is not unusual, even in fields such as environmental epidemiology or occupational health, where causal claims frequently remain contested despite long-term exposure patterns and consistent statistical associations. In the case of Agent Orange, the problem is exacerbated by the absence of key data, including precise spraying locations, exposure timing, individual susceptibility, pre-existing health conditions, and quantifiable dosage levels (McCulloch, 1984). As a result, researchers are often forced to rely on retrospective oral testimony, which is easily dismissed as unreliable.

Despite these constraints, the official scientific status of Agent Orange was effectively fixed by Judge Jack Weinstein's 1984 ruling, which held, on the basis of animal studies, that no definitive scientific proof existed linking Agent Orange to adverse health outcomes among US

---

[10] The American Association for the Advancement of Science (AAAS), which had helped to bring about the Mid-West Research Institute report, recommended an independent study carried out under the authority of the UN to ensure political impartiality. This was dismissed by the Department of State (McCulloch, 1984, p.82).

veterans (Schuck, 1986; McHugh, 2011). This position has remained largely unchanged. The logic underpinning this stance can be summarised as follows: because it has not been proven that we are wrong, we assume we are right until definitive proof emerges. This reasoning exemplifies an antinomy in a Kantian sense, where contradictory claims persist because neither can be conclusively demonstrated although internal logic seems coherent (Kant, 2003). Just as Kant criticised attempts to prove or disprove antinomic matters on empirical grounds or limited logic, the absence of definitive scientific proof has been treated as evidence of no harm, allowing responsibility to be indefinitely deferred by demanding an impossible standard of certainty.

This logic was consolidated through a series of US-commissioned assessments following rising concerns in the late 1960s, including reports by the Mid-West Research Institute (1967), Fred Tschirley (1968), the Society for Social Responsibility in Science (1969), the National Cancer Institute (1969), and the National Academy of Sciences (1970). These assessments emerged from an institutional context in which earlier official evaluations had focused primarily on military effectiveness rather than human health consequences. As a result, no baseline human health data were collected, and no systematic monitoring of civilian exposure was established, since the programme was never designed as a public health study (McCulloch, 1984, p. 24). While phrased differently, these reports consistently concluded that available evidence was insufficient to establish definitive harm.

Parallel research conducted in South Vietnam between 1960 and 1969, including the study *Congenital Malformations, Hydatidiform Moles and Stillbirths in the Republic of Vietnam* by R. T. Cutting and colleagues, similarly reported no statistically significant differences based on hospital maternity records (Cutting et al., 1970). These findings were later criticised for methodological weaknesses and unreliable data sources (Young and Reggiani, 1988). In the 1980s, the Vietnamese government established the 10–80 Committee to coordinate Agent Orange research, yet studies by Vietnamese epidemiologists were rarely published in international peer-reviewed journals due to methodological constraints (Schechter and Constable, 2006). Developing the capacity to measure toxic exposure levels requires substantial financial resources, estimated at around USD $1,000 per case (Kurlantzick, 2010)[11].

From the publication of the first commissioned scientific reports in 1967 onward, the core conclusion has remained strikingly stable: while some reports acknowledged indications of rising health problems following herbicide use, they consistently maintained that no definitive causal relationship could be established between Agent Orange exposure and human health damage, and almost invariably recommended further research. Over time, this position consolidated into an operational logic in which uncertainty itself became grounds

[11] Such scientific verification entails substantial financial and technical resources. By contrast, Agent Orange victims typically receive modest monthly assistance, often in the range of USD $50–100. This disparity highlights the opportunity cost of evidentiary demands that prioritise scientific verification over direct support for victims.

for continuation rather than restraint. In effect, the prevailing reasoning amounted to the claim that *"we do not know whether it is unsafe yet, so until we know for sure that it is unsafe, it is to be regarded as not unsafe."* This reasoning allowed the US government to justify continued use by placing decisive weight on institutional scientific authority rather than emerging signals of harm.

This position was articulated in the context of growing scientific opposition, including a petition signed by more than 5,000 scientists, among them 17 Nobel laureates, calling for an end to herbicide use. Subsequent criticism from the scientific community argued that such confidence was unjustified given the absence of evidence ruling out harm (Wolfle, 1989). Yet the inconclusive nature of scientific findings was repeatedly mobilised to frame herbicide use as unintentional and morally innocent. The National Academy of Sciences' final report (1974), for example, concluded that it was "unable to gather any definitive indication of direct damage by herbicides to human health," prioritising certainty over probability.

What this body of research achieved was not resolution, but the permanent suspension of accountability. By demanding definitive causality in a context where such proof is structurally unattainable, the credibility of the Agent Orange issue was effectively sealed as unresolved. Scientists who failed to establish direct causal links were not necessarily dishonest, as definitive conclusions may never be possible given missing data and long-term latency effects (d'Aquino, 2012). It was primarily US authorities who strategically mobilised this uncertainty to serve political interests. This manoeuvre has not gone unnoticed by victims, some of whom have responded with bitter irony: *"If it is not harmful, let US policymakers drink it."* Such remarks expose the absurdity of imposing impossible evidentiary burdens on those who bear the consequences of denial. However, in contrast to the US attitude, the Australian High Court's 1981 decision in favour of Vietnam veteran Nancy Law reveals an entirely different juridical logic (McCulloch, 2004, pp. 183–187). In this case, Justice Murphy ruled that the burden of disproof rests with the state, not the claimant, arguing that it is an error to require a prima facie case when the duty to disprove lies elsewhere. This legal reasoning marks a striking reversal of evidentiary responsibility.

An enormous amount of resources was used to justify herbicide use instead of assisting victims (Gough, 2002). Nevertheless, this only displaced the issue from political responsibility into the technical realms of toxicology and epidemiology. Yet one does not need advanced science to recognize harm when circumstantial evidence is so clear. Some have argued that proof of harm was attainable given contemporary knowledge, had there been political will (McCulloch, 1984, p.170). However, the Department of Veterans' Affairs responded with denial and hostility, disguising a political issue as scientific and abstract (p.193). Unlike US soldiers exposed to radiation during atomic testing in the 1950s and 1960s, for whom compensation was later granted on the basis of probabilistic causation, Vietnam veterans faced exceptional hurdles due to the wider socio-political implications of acknowledging responsibility (pp. 183–184).

This insistence on definitive proof is particularly ill-suited to carcinogenic, teratogenic, and mutagenic harms, which often manifest across generations and resist linear causal attribution. Controlling for confounding variables in contexts marked by war, poverty, displacement, and environmental degradation is methodologically impossible, rendering the demand for certainty a misalignment of scientific logic rather than a neutral standard. As Michael Gough, former head of the US Office of Technology Assessment, later reflected, Congress could have responded by providing medical care and compensation in the absence of conclusive causal evidence, grounding its decision in compassion and policy judgment rather than flawed scientific gatekeeping (Gough, 2003, p.196). In retrospect, the turn to science functioned less as a search for truth than as a means of deferring political accountability.

However, the establishment of the Presumptive Conditions List in 1991, and its continued expansion alongside advances in diagnostic technologies and epidemiological research, reflects the progressive recognition and institutional acceptance of causal links between Agent Orange exposure and specific health outcomes in the United States. The list specifies illnesses eligible for Agent Orange related compensation and has been periodically revised as new epidemiological findings and diagnostic capacities emerge[12], indicating that scientific evidence based on likelihood rather than certainty has been considered sufficient for institutional recognition within the US veterans' system (VA Claims

[12] The list started with 3 Agent Orange related illnesses identified and grew to include over 50 illnesses in 2025.

Insider, 2005). Rather than reflecting a one-off political settlement, the evolving nature of the list demonstrates a continuing process in which accumulating scientific knowledge has been translated into policy decisions regarding compensation.

Scientific discourse in the Agent Orange case serves a sovereign exception, exemplifying what Agamben (1995) describes as the fundamental impunity of sovereignty. By invoking scientific uncertainty and legal jurisdictional limits, the US government places Vietnamese victims in a "zone of indistinction," where suffering is acknowledged only as bare life, stripped of juridical and political standing. Acknowledging responsibility would risk opening broader claims related to civilian harm across other military interventions, a risk further contained through doctrines such as sovereign immunity that shield both the state and its contractors from accountability (Glaberson, 2004). In this sense, indemnification is not merely the absence of responsibility but an active exercise of sovereign authority, one that legitimises the power through the language of science and law.

2. Political and moral

Building on the preceding discussion of scientific discourse, this section examines how the entanglement of Agent Orange within Vietnam–US relations enabled the issue to shift from a matter of bilateral diplomacy into a structured deferral of moral responsibility. It begins by showing how both governments, guided by strategic restraint and diplomatic priorities, effectively muted public and political engagement with the Agent Orange legacy. As formal political and legal solutions remained unattainable, the issue was gradually displaced into the moral and humanitarian domain, where limited forms of assistance could be offered without confronting questions of accountability or liability. This reconfiguration allowed the appearance of ethical concern while preserving political deadlock, rendering victims present as objects of care but absent as autonomous agents. Tracing this trajectory reveals how political calculations repeatedly shaped, delayed, and redirected moral engagement, ensuring that responsibility was softened, deferred, or dissolved within broader frameworks of reconciliation and cooperation.

Diplomatic relations

The pervasiveness of Agent Orange discourse, in which one side claims millions of victims while the other denies any causal link, stems largely from persistent US insistence that no scientific evidence conclusively connects Agent Orange exposure to illness. This position has been central to producing a silenced and unresolved discourse, subsequently reinforced by political decisions shaped by the selective deployment of scientific authority on the US side and strategic compromise on the Vietnamese side. The resulting implicit agreement to consign the Agent Orange legacy to the past (d'Aquino et al., 2012) functions less as an articulation of historical truth than as a stabilising political arrangement, serving the diplomatic interests of both states.

During the period from 1975 to 1995, when diplomatic relations between Vietnam and the United States were suspended, the

Vietnamese Communist Party leadership remained nervous about the intentions of its former adversary and deliberately refrained from asserting outright victory over the United States in the war (Marr and White, 1988). This posture was reflected in the conciliatory language adopted by then–Foreign Minister Nguyễn Cơ Thạch, who stated in a 1988 interview that "both countries have been victims of war" and that "there are no losers and no winners," emphasising Vietnam's desire for peace and friendship with the United States rather than continued antagonism (*USA Today*, June 10, 1988, quoted in Marr and White 1988). Echoing this reconciliatory framing years later, Raymond Burghardt, former US ambassador to Vietnam, observed in 2002 that Agent Orange remained one of the most significant "ghosts" of the war, highlighting its persistent and unresolved presence in shaping bilateral relations between the two countries (Fox, 2007).

It was a strategic decision on Vietnam's part to avoid actions that might provoke the United States or draw renewed public attention to the contentious legacies of an unpopular war, so as not to jeopardise efforts to normalise bilateral relations. Vietnam's ambition to join the World Trade Organization and other international institutions, objectives that would not have been attainable without US support, further reinforced this restraint (Cane, 2010). Reflecting these priorities, both Vietnam and the United States showed reluctance to engage publicly with the Agent Orange issue. Available evidence suggests that when diplomatic relations were formally re-established in 1995, a key condition was Vietnam's agreement not to pursue compensation claims related to Agent Orange (Uesugi, 2011; Fox 2007,

2024). This understanding substantially narrowed the scope of the issue by framing insolvent legal litigation as the primary avenue of resolution, a stipulation that has continued to shape subsequent engagements with Agent Orange. This official framing of the Agent Orange discourse practically deprived the victims, who feel a sense of injustice, of space to articulate and express their desire that some form of accountability must exist.

Economic concerns also played a role in the silencing of Agent Orange discourse. Vietnamese officials feared that pressing the Agent Orange issue too far could tarnish the country's international image and undermine exports of agricultural and aquacultural products, which form the backbone of Vietnam's trade with the global market. As Martin (2012) notes, some government ministries were concerned that drawing sustained attention to dioxin contamination might not only complicate relations with the United States but also generate broader economic repercussions for Vietnam.

Beyond diplomatic and economic considerations, discursive asymmetries were also shaped by the uneven distribution of attention within the United States itself. In the United States, debates over the Vietnam War and Agent Orange focused primarily on US veterans and the safety of the domestic population, while Vietnamese victims received little attention. This imbalance contributed to a collective American psyche in which the suffering of Vietnamese victims remains marginal, making it difficult to establish a meaningful framework of recognition in the present day. Although the

Vietnamese public no longer view the United States as an enemy and are increasingly drawn to its cultural hegemony, many Americans continue to see Vietnam through the lens of an unpopular war and military failure[13] (Cane, 2010).

The official position of the United States has remained unchanged and was reaffirmed during the Bill Clinton administration, when Assistant Deputy Undersecretary of Defense Gary Vest made it clear that the United States would not admit responsibility. The same position was reiterated by Secretary of Defense Donald Rumsfeld and Secretary of Veterans Affairs Jim Nicholson. In 2016, during President Obama's visit to Vietnam, a meeting with Agent Orange victims was reportedly discussed but ultimately did not take place (Dung, 2023). Overall, there has been little change in the enduring silence surrounding Vietnamese victims within US official discourse.

The 2005 Lawsuit and VN Government Position

Following the normalisation of diplomatic relations with the United States in the mid-1990s, Vietnam grew more confident and gradually vocal on the Agent Orange issue. In the period leading up to the 2005 lawsuit filed in the US District Court in New York, Vietnamese victims pressed for compensation from the manufacturers of Agent Orange.

[13] One notable initiative addressing the Vietnamese war legacy was the establishment of the US–Vietnam Agent Orange Dialogue Group in 2007, sponsored by the Ford Foundation. The group brought together prominent figures, including former diplomats and policy experts, and aimed to draw attention to key actions required to address the legacy of Agent Orange. It was initially active, with Vietnamese members participating in roundtable discussions in the United States. However, the initiative later became inactive, with no clear explanation in the public record.

Since the move was technically initiated by Agent Orange victims rather than by the government, although the class action was coordinated by the Vietnam Association for Victims of Agent Orange/Dioxin (VAVA), the Vietnamese government saw an opportunity to pursue the issue and promote the cause unofficially. Prior to the trial, media coverage and publications on Agent Orange victims increased significantly, with the aim of raising public awareness and generating support. This effort gave rise to what was virtually a social movement, the "Struggle for Justice" (Dung, 2023). This included the US tour of Vietnamese female victims, who gave their testimonies to US media and engaged in public advocacy (Nhut, 2008).

Although no policy document explicitly states the government's position, the media mobilisation surrounding the lawsuit strongly suggests implicit state endorsement, given that Vietnam's media is largely state-owned and tightly controlled. After the US court dismissed the victims' claims, Vietnamese media expressed widespread public disappointment and anger. Nevertheless, the momentum generated around the lawsuit did not last much longer.

Those Vietnamese who had a little more insight into the issue discovered that affected American veterans were receiving government compensation[14] while Vietnamese claims were dismissed, leading to the logical lapses and anger that "those who sat on the

---

[14] In 2010, the US Congress allocated $13.3 billion for the affected US veterans and $12 million for Agent Orange relief in Vietnam (Nguyen & Hughes, 2017).

planes and spread toxics (American veterans) have been recognised as victims, while those who have had toxics spread over their heads have not[15]". It is difficult to gauge accurately the Vietnamese government's true stance and strategic positioning, as well as how actively it has pressed the issue. Nevertheless, Cane (2010) reveals that officials from the Ministry of Foreign Affairs, tasked with building the strategic relationship with the United States, have taken the most cautious approach. By contrast, conservatives within the ruling Communist Party, members of a pro-China faction and often the most sceptical of ties with the United States, have sought to push hardest on the Agent Orange issue and may strongly resist compromise.

Comparison with South Korea

While it is true that the Vietnamese government has, on several occasions, called on the United States to acknowledge responsibility, assessing whether this constitutes sufficient action is best understood through a comparative perspective. In this regard, South Korea's repeated and sustained demands on Japan over wartime crimes provide a useful point of reference, highlighting how state responsibility can be pursued as a long-term political strategy rather than as a sporadic moral appeal. This comparison also creates an opportunity to examine how the Agent Orange issue has unfolded within Vietnam's domestic political arena, in contrast to the international and diplomatic dynamics discussed above.

[15] Wording found at the display in the War Remnants Museum, Ho Chi Minh City.

There is no precise, officially tallied number of times that the South Korean government has requested an apology from the Japanese government for its wartime crimes. Nevertheless, clear patterns and distinct dynamics can be observed. The Japanese government has issued more than fifty statements of apology or remorse, often accompanied by the recurring question of how many times would be enough. These requests for apology have been multifaceted and persistent. In particular, whenever diplomatic tensions arise, such as controversies over Japanese school textbooks downplaying wartime crimes or visits by Japanese government officials to Yasukuni Shrine to honour war criminals, the victims' demands for apology tend to intensify.

Some apologies issued by Japanese prime ministers, notably the Kōno Statement in 1993 and the Murayama Statement in 1995, were deemed inadequate, leading to repeated demands from the South Korean government. These demands did not come solely from the state but also from parliament, non-governmental organisations, the media, and broader civil society, often through an unspoken collaboration between state actors and civil society groups. The relationship between government and civil society has been pivotal in raising issues the state itself considers politically "uncomfortable," as civil society can initiate collective public responses on the government's behalf, allowing the state to avoid direct diplomatic escalation.

However, a direct comparison between South Korea and Vietnam must be approached with caution. South Korea realised its democratic aspirations after decades of pro-democracy struggle across society, whereas Vietnam remains under the one-party rule of the Communist Party. This structural difference helps explain why, in the Vietnamese context, civil society has not been able to assume a comparable role. The contrast with South Korea highlights that the capacity of civil society to sustain pressure on the state is not simply a matter of moral resolve but is structurally conditioned by political regime and institutional design. This makes it necessary to examine the specific configuration of civil society in Vietnam and its implications for advocacy on issues such as Agent Orange.

Defining civil society and NGOs is inherently contentious, as inclusion and exclusion are shaped by local political and institutional conditions. Western-centric conceptions of civil society as a sphere of voluntary, autonomous, and self-generating social organisation independent of the state (Diamond, 1994) are of limited applicability to China and Vietnam, where assumptions about state–society relations and the roles assigned to civic actors differ fundamentally (Do, 2021). Estimates of the size of Vietnam's civil society vary widely, ranging from approximately 2,000 to 15,000 organisations (Civicus et al., 2006; Nguyen, 2022). Most domestic NGOs operate with limited resources, often on budgets below US$300,000, and are relatively new, capacity-focused, and constrained by limited public recognition and official understanding (Taylor, 2013).

More critically, the institutional role assigned to domestic NGOs significantly limits their advocacy potential. The vast majority are positioned as implementing partners of the state, primarily in welfare provision, social services, and poverty alleviation (Hannah, 2007). This functional alignment with state objectives curtails their capacity to act as independent watchdogs or agenda-setters, rendering their influence on contentious public issues, such as Agent Orange, structurally weak.

Vietnamese Civil Society

The regulatory and political constraints on civil society become more pronounced in the case of foreign NGOs operating in Vietnam. While the Vietnamese government has sought to benefit from the financial and technical resources foreign NGOs bring, it has simultaneously worked to minimise their political and social influence. Sidel (2023) observes that although foreign NGOs once operated under relatively flexible conditions during periods prioritising resource inflows, they have become increasingly subject to restrictive regulatory oversight. Foreign NGOs are prohibited from fundraising domestically, required to obtain prior approval for activities, and obligated to submit regular reports to state authorities.

Institutional control is exercised through multiple channels. The Committee for Foreign Non-Governmental Organization Affairs (COMINGO), under the Vietnam Union of Friendship Organizations, facilitates foreign NGO operations while simultaneously monitoring regulatory compliance (Vietnam Union of Friendship Organizations, n.d.; Vietnam.vn, n.d.). Although the Ministry of Foreign Affairs serves as the formal supervisory authority, security agencies maintain indirect oversight through monitoring local staff and information flows. As Sidel (2023) notes, existing laws have been mobilised to suppress dissent within civil society, alongside efforts to further tighten the legal framework governing NGOs.

These trends were consolidated with the issuance of Decree No. 58/2022/ND-CP, which significantly narrowed the scope of permissible foreign NGO activities while retaining broad prohibitions against actions deemed harmful to "national interests," "social order," "social ethics," "customs," or "national unity." Under such conditions, the prospects for sustained NGO-led monitoring or advocacy on behalf of Agent Orange victims remain severely constrained.

More generally, the relationship between NGOs and the state is inherently ambivalent. NGOs may act as watchdogs or collaborators depending on institutional context. In Vietnam, however, the subordination of NGOs under one-party rule has curtailed the organic development of civil society, limiting its capacity to amplify victim-centred narratives or challenge dominant state framings of Agent Orange. Instead, civil society engagement remains largely confined to reinforcing officially sanctioned positions.

Two additional institutions play a central role in shaping Agent Orange discourse: the media, which structures public visibility, and the Vietnam Association for Victims of Agent Orange/Dioxin (VAVA), which mediates advocacy and victim representation. Their roles are examined in later sections.

Humanitarian Aid as Political Deflection

The deadlock in diplomatic resolution and the inability to move the issue forward in the political domain shifted discussion of Agent Orange into the moral and humanitarian sphere. As Blattenberger (2016) notes, community attitudes toward the war and its legacy in Vietnam have gradually moved from an aggressive, accusatory tone to a more reconciliatory one, reflecting broader social changes in which the war is increasingly seen as distant, and the connection between war as ideology and individual identity is weakening. This shift is especially visible among the younger, postwar generation, for whom the war holds little relevance. In this context, the humanitarian framing of Agent Orange has gained prominence, yet it cannot be attributed solely to changing attitudes. From the outset, humanitarian discourse was strategically employed when political resolution seemed unreachable, serving as a pragmatic channel, and even a bargaining tool, for both countries to engage with each other. Thus, humanitarianism both reflected the evolving outlook of Vietnamese society and provided a viable means of addressing the issue.

Another important factor for the mobilisation of the humanitarian angle is the fact that Vietnam's strategic importance has grown significantly over the past decades (US Department of State, 2023). In particular, Vietnam's potential role for the United States in counterbalancing China's growing influence in the South China Sea has become increasingly critical. These developments facilitated the expansion of humanitarian aid. Such moves also helped to mitigate international criticism, albeit from limited sections of the international community, that Agent Orange represents a case of international injustice and an example of a great power bullying a smaller country (Blattenberger, 2016). While the United States' denial of responsibility has remained unchanged, it has nonetheless begun offering humanitarian assistance through the United States Agency for International Development (USAID), which unofficially targets Agent Orange victims under the broader and officially sanctioned category of people with disabilities.

USAID disability support for Vietnam officially began in 1989 through the Senator Patrick Leahy War Victims Fund and the Displaced Children and Orphans Fund, providing rehabilitative services, prosthetics, orthopaedic devices, and training (USAID, 2019). Between fiscal years 2007 and 2023, the United States allocated US$496.3 million, of which approximately US$336 million was directed toward environmental remediation at former airbases contaminated by Agent Orange residues, while US$139.3 million supported health and disability programmes. This assistance makes no explicit reference to Agent Orange victims as beneficiaries, thereby remaining consistent with the US position while deflecting criticism.

Field-level accounts nonetheless suggest that bureaucratic complexity and weak accountability at the point of service delivery often limit the effectiveness of assistance for the most vulnerable. Interviews with programme stakeholders indicate that local delivery partners operate within complex jurisdictional arrangements between donor requirements and Vietnamese authorities, creating governance gaps. Observers further note that service provision frequently prioritises meeting quantitative targets for donor reporting, producing high recorded outputs without necessarily translating them into meaningful improvements in beneficiaries' lives. In some programmes, a substantial proportion of mobility devices, including prosthetic and orthopaedic equipment, reportedly go unused or are returned due to problems of fit, adaptation, or maintenance, outcomes that are rarely captured in official reports. According to project-level assessments, in certain areas only around 10 per cent of registered beneficiaries are certified Agent Orange victims, although the actual number receiving services is likely higher due to limitations in victim certification procedures[16] (Dung, 2023).

The language of official discourse, which had long avoided explicit acknowledgement of Agent Orange victims, was partially revised in the *Consolidated Appropriations Act of 2023*, which states that funding is to be used "to assist persons with severe physical mobility, cognitive, or developmental disabilities: provided that such funds shall be prioritised to assist persons whose disabilities may be related to the use of Agent Orange and exposure to dioxin" (Consolidated Appropriations Act, 2023). This marked a significant shift in US legislative language concerning Agent Orange victims in Vietnam, although the provision stopped short of acknowledging US responsibility or involvement. The fragility of this linguistic and policy

[16] Based on VNAH report for a project in Tay Ninh, Binh Phouc and Dong Nai where 500 certified victims were assisted out of 5700.

shift became evident in early 2025, when a change in US executive priorities resulted in the temporary suspension of several United States Agency for International Development programmes, including environmental remediation at contaminated airbase sites. As reported by Berry-Jester and Murphy (2025), the suspension was reversed within weeks following warnings from US embassy officials that halting remediation mid-process could exacerbate environmental harm, particularly through the exposure of contaminated soil during the rainy season. The Vietnamese government formally expressed serious concern. Taken together, this episode illustrates how humanitarian commitments to Agent Orange victims remain vulnerable to shifting political calculations, even after limited recognition has been formally incorporated into legislation.

3. Selective and purposive

The preceding section traced how diplomatic deadlock and institutional arrangements shaped the international framing and delivery of US assistance. This section turns to the symbolic apparatus through which Agent Orange discourse has been domestically constructed in Vietnam. The analysis examines how meanings are selectively framed and circulated, producing a homogeneous humanitarian narrative centred on victimhood that simultaneously sustains a paradigm of national unity under one-party rule. In doing so, the section highlights the absence of pluralist debate and the ad hoc, state-directed character of discursive practice in Vietnam

There are several historical factors that form the background to the Agent Orange discourse in Vietnam. Unlike the Vietnam War, which officially ended in April 1975 with the powerful symbolic image of a tank entering the presidential palace thus conveying a sense of formal closure, the effects of Agent Orange were not recognised until almost two decades later. During the Vietnam War itself, the harmful effects of Agent Orange were not yet known. In some cases, the lack of awareness was so complete that people reportedly believed the spray to be mosquito repellent and deliberately ran towards it (Chae, 2013). The key attributes that define the Agent Orange issue, such as scientific evidence, jurisprudence, and civic and moral standards, have evolved continuously since the spraying of Agent Orange. This implies that the status of Agent Orange is largely dependent on discursive developments, which have been contingent on political events and subsequent discoveries.

However, for the Vietnamese public, engagement with this discursive construction has been restricted to responding in a largely unanimous manner through government-selected languages, which form the basic frame of the internal symbolic apparatus. For Agent Orange victims, this offers little ground on which to form their own narratives, as their most traumatic experiences remain subject to ongoing debate and are required to conform to what is permissible within the symbolic apparatus.

To clarify the selective character of discursive construction in Vietnam, it is useful to compare it with South Korea, where public discussion of wartime experiences has evolved in a more organic and pluralised manner. South Korea's involvement in the Vietnam War, and its postwar relationship with Vietnam, make this comparison particularly relevant. Most importantly, the Vietnamese government's handling of South Korea's wartime legacy exposes a broader strategic attitude toward war memory, which also shapes the selective framing of Agent Orange discourse in ways that reinforce national unity under one-party rule.

During the Vietnam War, South Korea was one of six countries that fought alongside the United States against North Vietnam. Under President Park Chung Hee, the South Korean government proposed sending troops to support the United States, which at the time faced considerable political pressure. Between September 1964 and March 1973, South Korea deployed approximately 300,000 soldiers to Vietnam, who conducted 563,387 military operations in high-risk areas. Drawing on combat experience from the Korean War (1950–1953), South Korean forces played a significant tactical role for the United States and operated in areas such as Phong Nhi and Phong Nhat in Quang Nam. However, subsequent investigations revealed that South Korean troops committed large-scale massacres of Vietnamese civilians in these regions. Korean court records document 1,384 cases of war crimes, including murder, rape, and manslaughter (Choi, 2007), while Vietnamese estimates suggest approximately 9,000 civilian deaths across some 80 massacres (Dung, 2022). These actions contributed to a reputation for combat effectiveness coupled with excessive brutality (Park, 2015).

These war crimes entered South Korean public discourse only in the 1990s, following investigations by progressive media, triggering intense debate. The issue was especially sensitive because South Korea had long demanded apologies from Japan for wartime atrocities, including the "comfort women[17]" issue. The revelation that Koreans were also perpetrators generated public pressure for an official apology to Vietnam, on the grounds that failure to do so would undermine South Korea's moral standing. Reflecting this sentiment, President Kim Dae-jung expressed his intention to apologise during a state visit to Vietnam (Parliament of Korea, 2023). The Vietnamese government, however, declined the offer.

Scholars identify four main reasons for this refusal (Lee, 2018). First, Vietnam's official narrative emphasises its status as the victor of the war; within this framework, victors do not seek apologies or compensation from defeated parties. Although Vietnam was unable to impose reparations, refraining from such claims was framed as preserving national dignity and unity, while downplaying victimhood that might complicate this image. Second, accepting a South Korean apology would have set a precedent for similar claims against other US allies involved in the war, such as Australia, New Zealand, and Thailand, creating diplomatic complexity the Vietnamese government sought to avoid. By recognising the United States as the

[17] Comfort women refers to women and girls who were coerced or forcibly taken into sexual servitude by the Japanese Imperial Army during the Asia–Pacific War (1930s–1945). They were confined in military-controlled brothels and subjected to repeated sexual violence. The term derives from the Japanese euphemism *ianfu* and is widely criticised for obscuring the coercive nature of what many scholars and human rights bodies identify as military sexual slavery.

sole official adversary and treating other participants as auxiliary forces, Vietnam maintained a contained bilateral narrative that preserved coherence in its war memory.

Third, Vietnam has promoted a pragmatic historical ethos encapsulated in the phrase "*forget the past and open a new future*" (*Khép lại quá khứ, hướng tới tương lai*), particularly after the adoption of Đổi Mới. This approach prioritises future cooperation over revisiting past atrocities and reflects concerns that governmental disputes over history could jeopardise economic relationships (Dung, 2022). South Korea's growing economic importance to Vietnam further reinforced this stance. When South Korean leaders publicly honoured Vietnam War veterans, Vietnamese reactions were muted or quickly suppressed by the state to prevent diplomatic escalation amid concerns over economic repercussions (Jung, 2017).

Fourth, the Vietnamese government remains deeply concerned about domestic social cohesion. The Vietnam War bore many characteristics of a civil war, leaving unresolved tensions between North and South that continue to shape postwar memory and reconciliation. Despite government efforts to promote national unity, unspoken resentment and hostility persist among segments of the population over wartime experiences on both sides. In this context, an official apology process or formal investigation into wartime atrocities could expose violence committed by multiple actors, potentially destabilising the fragile process of national reconciliation (Jung, 2016). Historical evidence underscores these sensitivities. Between 1957 and 1972, North

Vietnamese forces assassinated 36,725 and abducted 58,499 South Vietnamese, approximately 80 percent of whom were civilians (Lewy, 1980, pp. 272–273). US officials also acknowledged that both North and South Vietnamese forces often showed limited concern for civilian casualties; Robert Komer, who led the Phoenix Program[18], later recalled that Vietnamese forces on both sides were far less concerned about civilian casualties and damage than were the Americans (Trooboff, 1975, p. 99). In this sense, the government's relative passivity on the Agent Orange issue is closely linked to the broader imperative of maintaining postwar reconciliation between North and South.

Taken together, these dynamics reveal that Vietnam's selective handling of South Korea's wartime legacy is closely tied to its broader strategy of managing postwar reconciliation through controlled narratives. This approach helps explain the passivity and constraint surrounding the Agent Orange issue, where acknowledgement of harm is carefully balanced against the risks such recognition might pose to national unity.

The following paragraph outlines the unification process and its failures, drawing on Goscha's (2016, pp. 408–423) account. This background illustrates how the Vietnamese government has historically managed reconciliation through selective narratives rather

---

[18] *Chiến dịch Phụng Hoàng* A program implemented by the US during the last years of American involvement in Vietnam designed to identify and destroy Viet Cong political infrastructure by means of assassination, capture, and torture of civilian suspects. 26369 were killed under the program. (Andrade & Willbanks 2006).

than open confrontation with internal divisions. Examining this process is necessary because the state-managed framing of reunification established a discursive framework for governing other politically sensitive legacies, including Agent Orange. These dynamics help explain why reconciliation remains a vulnerable and sensitive issue for national unity, continuing to shape the discourse on Agent Orange.

The victory of April 30, 1975, was achieved not by the North Vietnamese army alone but through a coalition of the People's Army of Vietnam (PAVN) and the National Liberation Front (NLF), which included non-communist southerners. Although the Paris Accords of 1973 envisaged a coalition government and temporary two-state coexistence pending national elections, these provisions were abandoned after the fall of Saigon. Hanoi quickly disarmed the South and absorbed it under full control. No elections were held, no coalition formed, and no autonomous South Vietnam remained. Tens of thousands of northern cadres were dispatched to assume authority, turning unification into a swift takeover rather than the gradual reconciliation many had anticipated.

Consolidation was enforced through political and ideological measures. Re-education camps detained former officials and soldiers; self-criticism sessions and propaganda campaigns were mandated; schools and workplaces promoted hero worship; and cultural erasure took place through the closure of media outlets, renaming of streets, and destruction of monuments. These measures homogenized the population politically and ideologically, leaving no room for pluralist voices. Economic policies added to the hardship: collectivization reduced productivity, commercial networks were confiscated, and more than 200,000 ethnic Chinese fled. By the late 1970s, famine and economic collapse gripped the South, while over 800,000 "boat people" fled abroad, stark evidence of failed reconciliation.

Despite these crises, Vietnam endured as one system and later stabilized through Đổi Mới. The government's official narrative, however, frames unification as a shared triumph for all, erasing experiences of repression and displacement (Grossheim, 2021). This celebratory account established a precedent for state-managed memory: reconciliation defined only on official terms[19]. The same selective framing, emphasizing unity while silencing discord, would later shape the discourse on Agent Orange.

For these reasons, when a Korean president makes an official visit to Vietnam and the issue of a formal apology resurfaces, both governments typically settle on the diplomatic phrasing of an "expression of regret." It is against this backdrop that the issue of Agent Orange must be understood, situated at the intersection of contested boundaries where responsibility is displaced into technical

---

[19] Even today, unresolved tensions from the civil war surface in everyday discourse. Although open regional criticism is largely taboo in Vietnam, such sentiments continue to circulate informally within regional networks (Song, 2018). This tension is sometimes expressed through popular humour: a common piece of popular satire suggests that genuine national unity was achieved not in 1975 but symbolically in 2018, when a South Korean coach led the national football team to victory, momentarily uniting northern and southern players—an anecdote that ironically highlights the absence of comparable reconciliation in political life.

and administrative disputes. US policymakers, for example, frequently portrayed the Vietnam War as a large-scale counterinsurgency more akin to a civil war than an act of foreign aggression (McCulloch, 1984, p. 51). At one point, the US government even argued that the decision to deploy Agent Orange originated with the South Vietnamese government (McCulloch, 1984, p. 21).

Historical records indicate that in 1961 a feasibility test was conducted at the joint American–South Vietnamese Combat Development Test Centre, resulting in a request to the US Department of State to authorise use of Agent Orange, a herbicidal defoliant to strip forest cover and destroy crops (Hopton & Walton, 2018). Early missions included a South Vietnamese Air Force flight commander on board, and President Ngô Đình Diệm's government actively supported the programme (McCulloch, 1984, pp. 20, 30). Defoliant operations were welcomed by the South Vietnamese authorities for their perceived tactical advantages, including the displacement of rural populations from Viet Cong strongholds (McCulloch, 1984, p. 25). Records further show that even after the conclusion of Operation Ranch Hand (1961–1971), small-scale defoliant missions continued to be carried out by the South Vietnamese army (McHugh, 2011).

In the absence of a settled political or legal resolution, the Agent Orange issue has been increasingly mobilised as a site for fostering social cohesion and national harmony. The stories of Agent Orange victims and their families in Vietnam are framed primarily to appeal to public compassion and to build solidarity across diverse communities. Mass media coverage frequently promotes fundraising campaigns and encourages participation in nationwide efforts to support victims. Whereas the experience of war itself was deeply divisive, dismantling social bonds at both individual and collective levels, the Agent Orange issue, inflicted by a foreign power, paradoxically unites the country and carries a healing social and political effect. This produces a further paradox: although Vietnam is internationally recognised as the victorious side of the war, the continued emphasis on victimhood surrounding Agent Orange binds these victims within a humanitarian narrative that suspends their claims in a prolonged political limbo. Media outlets play a central role in generating shared emotions of pain and sympathy by portraying victims not only as southerners or Kinh, but also as northerners and ethnic minorities. These representations are often accompanied by vivid images that evoke sadness and compassion, leading audiences to the conviction that collective action is necessary (Khong Dien, 2006; Fox, 2007; Gammeltoft, 2014).

However, assistance to Agent Orange victims remains a contested domain. Although official policy presents support as humanitarian and inclusive, in practice the Vietnamese government's assistance operates in a selective and uneven manner. Support is prioritised for victims recognised as having rendered "meritorious service," primarily those who served in the North Vietnamese forces and their families (Dung, 2023). By contrast, individuals associated with the South are generally limited to standard disability pensions, which provide substantially lower monthly support. As a result, a programme framed as humanitarian and unifying reproduces differentiated access to care and compensation. In this sense, the assistance regime contradicts the discourse of national solidarity it publicly promotes. Limited transparency and discretionary practices within the bureaucratic system produce outcomes that are formally inclusive yet substantively discriminatory in effect.

4. Lack/denial of victims' agency

Within the symbolic apparatus of Vietnamese discourse, Agent Orange victims are positioned primarily as objects of humanitarian concern rather than as political subjects. Their representation is dominated by a discourse of victimhood that denies them political agency, reducing them to passive recipients of compassion instead of acknowledging them as actors capable of exercising political rights. In media and public narratives, victims are frequently objectified through images of bodily deformity, framed as humanitarian tragedy or as the destructive aftermath of war inflicted by powerful external forces. As a result, Agent Orange victims are portrayed less as citizens with political voice and more as symbolic embodiments of the damage war inflicts on humanity.

In major Vietnamese cities, Agent Orange victims are often encountered directly in everyday urban spaces. It is not uncommon to see individuals pushing small carts fitted with portable karaoke speakers, singing beneath pedestrian overpasses while displaying handwritten signs identifying themselves as Agent Orange victims and requesting donations. These encounters place suffering in immediate proximity to the public, bypassing mediated representation. Yet this visibility is uneven. Victims with milder impairments and verbal capacity may articulate emotion, resilience, or hope and are therefore more readily incorporated into media narratives. By contrast, those with severe deformities and no means of communication[20] are rendered visible only through the public gaze, which is frequently marked by shock, discomfort, or silent pity rather than engagement.

In some instances, victims are presented as symbols of resistance and hope, often in a clichéd and depoliticised manner. As one exhibition description notes, "Agent Orange victims have been transformed from the broken physical state of their bodies to exist on a higher plane, transcending their biological circumstances to live and thrive" (photo exhibition description, Blattenberger 2016, p. 31). Overall, it is rare for the public to encounter Agent Orange victims articulating their own views or exercising political voice regarding the disabilities imposed on their bodies and the impact on their lives (BBC Monitoring, 2004). Agent Orange victims have been the subject of relatively few qualitative field studies in which their narratives are recorded and analysed as primary data. While such studies create limited opportunities for victims' voices to be heard, these voices are typically

[20] The Vietnamese Red Cross estimates that at least 150,000 children in Vietnam live with severe disabilities believed to be associated with Agent Orange exposure, many of whom suffer from profound cognitive and physical impairments that severely limit or prevent their ability to communicate (cited in USIP, 2022).

mediated through researchers' analytical frameworks, with specific aspects of lived experience selected and organised in accordance with research objectives rather than victims' own priorities.

Moreover, interviews with victims are almost invariably conducted in the presence of local authority representatives, a condition that constrains the expression of honest opinions and effectively precludes open criticism of government policy. This structural mediation produces a form of speech that is cautious, partial, and often reduced to expressions of suffering rather than political judgment.

As Žižek argues in relation to traumatic experience more broadly, including Holocaust narratives, victims cannot fully describe their suffering in an "adequate" or "accurate" manner within the symbolic order of intersubjective communication (Žižek, 2012). Trauma exceeds available symbolic frameworks, meaning that what is most essential to the experience resists articulation and appears instead as fragmentation, repetition, or silence. This does not indicate a failure on the part of victims, but rather a structural limit of language and representation itself. Consequently, the absence of political articulation should be understood in relation to structural and institutional constraints on expression rather than as an individual deficiency.

It is therefore very rare for Agent Orange victims to express views on *how* the issue should be addressed at the level of policy or justice. This is often interpreted as a lack of understanding of the broader political context and of possible courses of action. However, effective advocacy requires specific forms of mediation, including the articulation of demands, the formation of support networks, negotiation with key stakeholders, and engagement in public education. Such processes require an interlocutor capable of translating suffering into political claims (Žižek, 2012, p. 29).

In the Vietnamese context, Agent Orange victims largely lack such interlocutors. Even where advocacy structures exist, victims' extreme poverty and unstable livelihoods leave little time or capacity for political engagement beyond daily low-paid labour (Dung, 2023). As a result, Agent Orange victims remain largely invisible as political subjects, occupying a position of enforced passivity that sharply distinguishes them from other categories of war victims who have been more successfully integrated into public, legal, and moral discourse.

This absence of mediation becomes particularly visible in recent efforts to pursue legal accountability beyond the Agent Orange context. In the 2023 lawsuit brought by Vietnamese victims against the Korean army for its role in the Quảng Nam massacre (VN Express, 2023), the plaintiffs relied primarily on Korean NGOs and civil society actors for legal representation, organisational coordination, and public advocacy. No Vietnamese organisation played a comparable facilitating role. The case therefore reveals not merely a cross-border legal initiative, but a structural gap within Vietnam's own civic infrastructure. Where sustained advocacy requires translation of suffering into legal claims, media engagement, and strategic mobilisation, domestic intermediaries capable of performing this function remain limited. The absence of such actors reinforces the broader pattern in which victims' grievances struggle to circulate beyond humanitarian framing and into sustained political or juridical discourse.

To illustrate this point further, the case of the Korean 'comfort women', another war victim group from the Second World War, provides a useful contrast. Despite the elapsed time of nearly eighty years since the end of the war, surviving comfort women have remained publicly visible and politically active, participating in sustained advocacy efforts both domestically and internationally. Crucially, their claims have been continuously mediated through legal action, civil society organisations, transnational activism, and symbolic public interventions. One prominent example is the ongoing 'Statue of Peace' movement, through which bronze statues representing young comfort women have been installed in major cities worldwide as part of a coordinated global public awareness campaign (ABC, 2016). Through such mechanisms, comfort women have been constituted as enduring political subjects within public, legal, and moral discourse, in sharp contrast to the relative invisibility of Vietnamese Agent Orange victims.

In South Korea, this visibility is sustained through continuous public engagement. Media coverage regularly reports on advocacy activities and closely tracks the number of surviving victims, reflecting widespread concern over the impending loss of living witnesses.

Weekly demonstrations held in front of the Japanese embassy in Seoul, ongoing since 1992, have taken place more than 1,500 times and continue to attract consistent public participation. Central to these campaigns are victims' personal testimonies, through which elderly survivors recount their experiences of sexual violence, anchoring the movement's moral and political claims in lived experience. Although the events occurred nearly eighty years ago, the war memory remains persistent, with survivors describing the injustice as ongoing rather than historical (Das & Kleinman, 2000; Chizuko, 1999). These testimonies have mobilised international support, contributing to resolutions and recommendations issued by multiple United Nations human rights bodies since 1994 (Center for Korean Legal Studies, 2022). Alongside successful domestic fundraising, the movement has fostered shared public sympathy and respect for victims' courage in speaking out, contrasting with the stigma and silencing that often characterise other contexts of wartime victimhood.

Korean victims believe that such acknowledgement can deliver justice and help relieve the ongoing psychological pain inflicted upon them. Although the events took place eighty years ago, the war memory remains torturous and difficult to detach from (Das and Kleinman, 2000), and for them the war crime is continuing (Chizuko, 1999). Vivid testimonies of sexual violence have drawn international supporters, forming alliances that have led to resolutions and recommendations by various UN human rights bodies and treaties since 1994 (Center for Korean Legal Studies 2022). Domestic fundraising campaigns have also been successful, but more importantly, there is a shared sympathy for their suffering and a respect for their courage in speaking out, rather than the stigma and victimisation that often silences victims elsewhere.

In contrast to the South Korean "comfort women" successful campaign, efforts in Vietnam have largely taken the form of appeals to sympathy for suffering victims. Public attention remains focused on representations of victimhood, with limited space for victims to organise collectively or assert themselves as political agents in claiming rights. As a result, Agent Orange victims tend to appear as research subjects, images, or statistics, and apart from individual acts of soliciting donations, do not constitute an organised social action or movement. Public discourse generally recognises them as casualties of an unfortunate past rather than as people continuing to live with ongoing psychological pain and distress that could be alleviated through greater public recognition and support. The disparity between the two cases highlights the role of pluralist political infrastructures in enabling sustained advocacy. Vietnam lacks the institutional conditions that made the Korean campaign possible, including support networks and coalitions that allow victims to speak out and develop strategies for public engagement. In pluralist societies, such networks are sustained by NGOs, media, religious organisations, and student movements. The "comfort women" campaign, for example, drew strength from women's organisations, mainstream and independent media, religious leaders across denominations, and a large student base whose activism carried forward the legacies of the pro-democracy movements of the 1980s and 1990s. It was this collective support that enabled elderly survivors, now in their eighties and nineties, to sustain advocacy efforts both domestically and internationally.

When multiple actors with distinct institutional and political interests participate in a support network, their positions may diverge, making it necessary to examine how victim narratives are mediated and translated into public claims. In the case of the "comfort women," supportive networks functioned as effective interlocutors by sustaining channels through which victims' testimonies could enter legal, political, and moral discourse without being reduced to humanitarian assistance or symbolic representation. Victims' testimonies thus operated not simply as personal accounts of suffering, but as statements that could be taken up, reiterated, and acted upon within broader structures of advocacy. By contrast, Vietnamese Agent Orange victims remain largely embedded within representations that speak *about* them rather than *with* them. In the absence of functioning interlocutors, such as independent NGOs, media platforms, religious organisations, and student alliances, their narratives are rarely translated into sustained political claims, reinforcing their positioning as objects of humanitarian concern rather than participants in shaping justice or policy.

The following section examines how the limited visibility of victim agency in Vietnam is shaped primarily through the roles of media and non-governmental organisations, particularly the Vietnam Association for Victims of Agent Orange (VAVA). These two actors play a central role in framing how Agent Orange victims are represented in public discourse and how their suffering is communicated to domestic and international audiences. Rather than serving merely as channels for victims' voices, media and NGOs function as key mediators that structure what can be said, how it can be said, and for what purposes. As a result, understandings of "victimhood" are largely produced through institutional narratives rather than articulated directly by victims themselves. This section therefore focuses on how media representations and NGO advocacy practices shape the boundaries of victim agency in the contemporary discourse on Agent Orange.

Media

According to the World Press Freedom Index published by Reporters Without Borders, Vietnam ranked 7th from the bottom in 2024, an improvement from 4th in 2021. Countries such as North Korea, Iran, and Afghanistan ranked below Vietnam, while Vietnam's position is even lower than China's. Media plays a critical role in forming public discourse and public consensus through the circulation of stories. In Vietnam, however, the media has long been disciplined to recognise its primary role as disseminating government information and propagating official narratives, rather than monitoring public affairs, examining government policies, or giving expression to the voices of individuals and social groups. Around one hundred editors-in-chief, all members of the Communist Party, attend weekly meetings at the Ministry of Information and Communications to coordinate media content and ensure alignment with Party media policy and the broader state apparatus (Hayton, 2010).

Media coverage of Agent Orange victims in Vietnam fluctuates in frequency. Attention tends to surge following specific events, such as international lawsuits, but overall coverage remains sporadic, with a clear long-term trend of fading media attention. The manner in which these stories are reported is largely homogeneous. Coverage focuses predominantly on the daily hardships of victims and their families, occasionally accompanied by moral commentary on injustice. These portrayals emphasise suffering and sympathy, yet they rarely move beyond descriptive accounts of hardship to generate sustained public debate or political discussion.

A comparison with media coverage of the "comfort women" issue in South Korea highlights both similarities and critical differences. In both cases, media narratives foreground victims' personal experiences. However, a major distinction lies in the political orientation of the coverage. In South Korea, media reporting explicitly calls for public support not merely in the form of material assistance, but as part of an ongoing struggle for justice led by the victims themselves. Victims openly criticise the inaction of their own government and directly target foreign governments over responsibility. This media environment has contributed to sustained political mobilisation, most visibly through the weekly demonstrations in front of the Japanese embassy in Seoul. Such practices have kept the issue present in public consciousness with a persistent sense of urgency.

In contrast, portrayals of Agent Orange victims in Vietnam are largely situated within a humanitarian frame. Media narratives tend to focus on life hardship and moral suffering, with limited extension into political action or policy debate. Compassion and sympathy are foregrounded, while claims-making or explicit demands for accountability remain marginal. This mode of representation aligns with broader media tendencies in Vietnam, where the poor have often been portrayed in hostile terms, framed as potential threats to public health and public order (Lincoln, 2014). Against this background, coverage of Agent Orange victims frequently emphasises their resilience and capacity to contribute economically and socially, highlighting productivity rather than structural injustice. Such representations present victims as non-burdens on society, sustaining moral sympathy while keeping the issue within socially and politically acceptable boundaries.

When Agent Orange was first reported in the US media during and shortly after the Vietnam War, it provoked strong public reactions and placed significant pressure on the US government, becoming a key factor in questioning the legitimacy of the US role in the war. In contemporary US media, however, the issue is rarely reported, except in connection with new scientific findings linked primarily to US veterans' campaigns. Coverage overwhelmingly focuses on American victims, failing to establish connections with Vietnamese victims and contributing to widespread unawareness among the US public regarding Vietnamese suffering (Lindorff, 2010).

Stainman (2021), a US journalist with extensive experience reporting from Vietnam since the Vietnam War, observes that despite occasional coverage, Agent Orange and its victims are increasingly underreported. Media attention has declined largely because there are no new developments, indicating that the issue has stalled without meaningful resolution. In this sense, the absence of "newsworthiness" reinforces the ongoing marginalisation of Vietnamese victims within both domestic and international media landscapes.

Vietnamese Association of Victims of Agent Orange (VAVA)

The Vietnamese Association for Victims of Agent Orange (VAVA) was established in 2004, shortly before the 2005 Vietnamese Agent Orange victims' court case in the United States, with the stated mission of assisting victims and their families through self-support, mutual support, and community support. The organisation coordinates assistance from other organisations and individuals and presents itself as an official representative voice for Agent Orange victims. While VAVA's dedication to assisting victims is widely recognised, its role in addressing victims' needs, particularly in articulating their voices, remains limited. The organisation's mission statement is broadly framed and does not explicitly identify advocacy as a central function. Instead, VAVA's activities have focused primarily on the delivery of government subsidies and the provision of community-based assistance programs, positioning the organisation largely within a welfare-oriented framework.

Despite its formal classification as a non-governmental organisation, VAVA operates in ways that closely resemble state agencies. Within the sector, this NGO designation is widely understood as a technical rather than substantive distinction. VAVA was conceived primarily as a mechanism to "socialise" aid funding, meaning that it mobilises resources from the public and external donors while operating under the direction of the state. In practice, this has positioned the organisation less as an independent civil agency and more as an intermediary extending state welfare functions. Its leadership structure reflects this proximity: VAVA directors are typically retired senior military officers appointed through government channels. As a result, the organisation functions within clearly defined political boundaries, limiting its capacity to act autonomously or to advance positions that diverge from official narratives.

Beyond its institutional status, VAVA also encounters significant difficulty in establishing and maintaining sustained connection with the Agent Orange victim community. Its manpower and administrative capacity are severely limited in relation to the geographical scope of its target population, which often includes remote and rural areas. Access is further constrained by social stigma surrounding Agent Orange, as many families do not wish to be identified publicly for fear of discrimination and long-term disadvantage to other family members. In remote areas, many families are occupied with agricultural labour or low-paid work during daytime hours, leaving little opportunity for engagement. Moreover, repeated interactions with researchers, journalists, and visiting delegations have generated fatigue among family members, particularly where testimonies, photographs, and interviews have produced no tangible improvement in living conditions. As Walton and Hopton (2018, p. 45) note, such encounters have often resulted in exhaustion rather than meaningful support. This sentiment is echoed in Fox's (2004) fieldwork, where community members observe that "*we have been back and forth many times raising hopes but the victims have not seen any results to date*" (p. 15), and that "*so many delegations have come here but we still haven't seen any help at all for the families' difficulties*" (p. 53). These conditions collectively limit VAVA's ability to act as an effective intermediary, constraining sustained communication and weakening its capacity to maintain durable relationships with victims and their families.

Taken together, these institutional characteristics, operational constraints, and representational practices point to a broader biopolitical function performed by the Vietnamese Association for Victims of Agent Orange. Rather than operating as an advocacy body that enables victims to articulate political claims or contest responsibility, VAVA functions primarily as a technical intermediary concerned with the management of suffering. Victims are rendered visible through categories of need, hardship, and rehabilitation, and their social value is framed in terms of care, resilience, and potential economic contribution. This representational logic is made explicit in VAVA's own communicative framing, where, as Walton & Hopton (2018, p. 29) note, a representative explains: "*We want to provoke pity, but from the pity the public may become motivated to help them (AO victims).*" Within this logic, victimhood becomes a governable condition to be alleviated through welfare provision and social support, rather than a basis for rights-based mobilisation. The emphasis on compassion, national solidarity, and social harmony reinforces this orientation, privileging stability and cohesion over political contestation. As a result, the articulation of victims' voices remains mediated and contained within humanitarian discourse, leaving little space for advocacy that might recognise Agent Orange victims as autonomous political subjects capable of acting upon their own rights.

Analysis of Agent Orange discourse

What began as a comparative observation during the author's time living in Vietnam, namely that Agent Orange was rarely spoken about in everyday conversation, is now empirically confirmed by the data. Drawing on the coded dataset, this section examines how silence, institutional framing, and biopolitical rationalities structure the representation of Agent Orange and its victims. Four interrelated themes organise the analysis, derived from the coding process and refined through cross-analysis of victim and institutional materials.

Theme 1: Silence, Asymmetry, and the Absence of Victim Voice

Theme 2: Symbolic Misalignment Between Lived Suffering and Institutional Meaning

Theme 3: Biopolitics, Science, and the Management of Life

Theme 4: Publics, Mediation, and the Failure of Narrative Circulation

Theme 1: Silence, Asymmetry, and the Absence of Victim Voice

A prevailing silence surrounds Agent Orange, and this silence itself functions as a form of discourse. At the social level, this silence is sustained through stigma and taboo. As one victim explains (entry # 3), "*There are a lot of families that don't want to welcome VAVA because if they talk openly, people will know there is an AO victim in their family... the family will suffer.*" This statement illustrates how stigma operates at the level of the family, where disclosure exposes households to reputational damage and social exclusion, thereby discouraging open acknowledgment of Agent Orange. Silence, in this sense, is not voluntary but socially imposed, extending beyond individual victims to shape broader community behaviour.

This socially enforced silence, however, cannot be understood solely as a matter of taboo or reluctance to speak. At a deeper structural level, it reflects a fundamental divergence between the meanings victims draw from their lived experiences and the dominant state and institutional discourses, including those of international stakeholders. While victims' narratives are grounded in embodied suffering and relational loss, official discourse remains depersonalised, technocratic, and developmental in orientation. The contrast is stark and enduring, producing a decades-long silence that is embedded within the structure of representation itself. As another victim states, "*I have tried to seek help, but no one listens. I feel invisible*" (entry #4), revealing not merely neglect but the structural absence of a listening position within the symbolic order.

This absence reflects a broader configuration in which the institutional and discursive frameworks that organise meaning, what Jacques Lacan (1994) conceptualises as the symbolic order or "Big Other", fail to recognise victims as speaking subjects. Within this structure, victims' experiences do not enter discourse as meaningful claims but are either excluded altogether or re-coded in ways that strip them of their original significance.

In contrast, the material reality of Agent Orange, bodily deformity, chronic illness, intergenerational damage, and irreversible loss, persists as what Lacan terms the Real: a dimension of lived experience that exceeds and resists full symbolisation. This produces a structural gap between lived suffering and its representation, where what is most concrete and immediate in victims' lives cannot be adequately translated into the languages of science, policy, or development. Rather than confronting this limit, dominant discourse operates through stabilising narratives that defer recognition and responsibility, allowing this gap to endure while maintaining the coherence of the broader system.

Entry #19 *"I blamed myself for decades until I learned that 'the poison Agent Orange' was the true culprit"* reveals the profound psychological and epistemic costs that structural silence imposes on Agent Orange victims. This silence operates not only at the level of public discourse but also within the formation of subjective understanding. The speaker, Tran To Nga, who lost her newborn child to heart defects, internalised the tragedy as personal failure for many years before situating it within the broader history of chemical exposure. Like many other victims, she interpreted misfortune as individual responsibility rather than as the consequence of toxic warfare. Victims endured the effects of Agent Orange long before they possessed the knowledge to situate their experience within a broader historical and political framework. It was only retrospectively, once the term "Agent Orange" became available as a name for the cause, that personal misfortune could be reinterpreted as inherited injury.

Although the Vietnamese state had publicly condemned Agent Orange, the prolonged refusal of the United States to acknowledge responsibility for its harmful health effects, combined with enduring community stigma surrounding disability and reproductive loss, created conditions in which a stable discursive frame had not yet taken form at the level of everyday life. In this environment, there existed no socially secure form through which private suffering could be articulated as collective injustice. The delayed recognition of the health effects of Agent Orange was shaped by multiple factors, including fragmented scientific knowledge in earlier decades, uneven medical communication, generational latency of symptoms, and the moralisation of disability within local communities. Under such circumstances, suffering was internalised rather than politicised, revealing not merely ignorance but the absence of an available symbolic form capable of transforming embodied pain into publicly recognised harm.

The critical discourse analysis reveals a strong tendency for Agent Orange to be spoken *about* rather than spoken *by* those most directly affected. Discursive processes have been largely dominated by state, institutional, and international actors, who establish the broader frameworks within which meaning is produced, while Agent Orange victims themselves have had little opportunity to function as producers of signifiers. This tendency was evident during the data collection process. The primary aim in selecting data for the victims' cohort was to identify as many first-person voices as possible, in the form of direct quotations, in which Vietnamese Agent Orange victims articulate what Agent Orange means to them and how it has shaped their lives. Despite intensive search efforts, including the use of advanced search tools, locating first-person direct quotations from Vietnamese Agent Orange victims proved difficult, underscoring the scarcity of victims' own voices within the existing discursive landscape.

The consequences of this discursive asymmetry extend beyond political marginalisation to the level of personal sense-making. When no stable public language is available through which suffering can be narrated as historically produced harm, individuals are left to interpret their experiences within private or moral frameworks. The absence of an accessible narrative form deprives victims of the opportunity to situate their pain within a coherent social history, limiting the development of self-understanding and collective memory. Without recognition, suffering remains fragmented rather than narratively integrated. This deprivation is not merely communicative but ontological: the inability to articulate harm as part of a shared story constrains the formation of political subjectivity itself. In this sense, silence does not simply prevent speech; it interrupts the conditions under which meaning, identity, and agency can take form.

This structural condition reflects a deeper limitation in how meaning is organised and made available within the discourse. In Lacanian terms, this configuration reveals the presence of a missing signifier within the discourse (Lacan, 2007). There exists no stable symbolic position from which either victims or the broader public can emerge as fully articulated speaking subjects. Although VAVA appeals to values already held by the public, seeking to mobilise compassion, *"We want to provoke pity, but from the pity they may become better motivated to help AO victims"* (entry # 77), it does not open a space for public participation in collective deliberation or discursive contestation. The public is thus mobilised affectively but not symbolically authorised to speak. Meanwhile, although VAVA's interactions with victims often centre on relational care and emotional support, these relationships remain outside the political register, operating through paternalistic assistance rather than recognition of victims as subjects of speech. As a result, both groups remain structurally muted: the public is presumed but not consulted, while victims are incorporated into networks of care yet denied a position within political articulation. Silence here is not simply the absence of words, but the absence of a recognised place from which speech can carry force.

Theme 2: Symbolic Misalignment Between Lived Suffering and Institutional Meaning

Building on the structural absence of a recognised speaking position outlined above, the data further reveal how this absence is actively organised within institutional discourse. Rather than simply reflecting a difference in perspective, the divergence between victims' lived suffering and dominant forms of meaning is structured through specific modes of classification, translation, and administrative framing. In this sense, the operation of biopolitical governance, as articulated by Michel Foucault, becomes visible not as an abstract principle but as a set of practices through which suffering is reformulated into measurable, manageable, and policy-relevant categories. While victims' accounts remain grounded in embodied experience, institutional discourse selectively translates these experiences into forms that can be recorded, evaluated, and acted upon within bureaucratic systems. What emerges, therefore, is not merely a gap between two perspectives, but a process in which lived experience is systematically reconfigured in order to fit the requirements of governance.

Although both victims' speech and state interpretation share a common historical origin, namely the legacy of dioxin exposure, their meanings unfold on separate planes. The dataset reveals not merely divergence but a persistent gap between two discursive realities that rarely intersect. The Agent Orange victim speaks in search of recognition, attempting to enter a system of meaning already shaped by the state's developmental and biopolitical narrative. Institutional discourse, by contrast, organises suffering into legible forms such as cases, statistics, and plans of remediation. The victim's voice is not denied outright but translated into signifiers that can be absorbed without disrupting the state's agenda. What remains unarticulated is not the voice itself but its excess, that which cannot be fully signified within available language. This excess points to dimensions of suffering that resist institutional interpretation, leaving a residue that cannot be incorporated into official discourse.

This difference becomes even clearer when comparing direct testimony from victims with official or institutional statements. In the Vietnamese dataset, one mother expressed a modest and concrete need that captures the logic of immediacy shaping victims' discourse: *"We hope that our child can be recognised as a victim of Agent Orange so that, when hospitalised, the financial burden on our family can be reduced"* (VN entry #10). The statement does not invoke legal responsibility, compensation, or geopolitical framing, but focuses narrowly on easing the conditions of everyday survival.

A similar register appears in interview material recorded by Fox (2024, pp. 28–29, 129–130), which offers a useful point of comparison. When asked what he wanted, a young man whose father served in an area sprayed with Agent Orange replied: *"I've seen that in this world there are other people like myself, but they have means to get around. If I want to go out on the street, go to my grandparents... to make it less sad... my father has to carry me... so I would like to ask for a way to get around."* When the mother of a young victim was asked what she needed, her response echoed the same logic of immediacy: *"I would like a hearing aid for my son. It's 800,000 VND (around US$30); for you it is not much, but for me it is impossible."*

These statements are direct, concrete, and focused on immediate improvements in quality of life. They do not rely on geopolitical frameworks, legal claims, or diplomatic recognition, and instead quietly call into question whether resolving the Agent Orange issue truly requires further decades of bilateral negotiation between the Vietnamese and US governments to address these immediate needs. As signifiers, the voices of the young man and the mothers who want the means to get around and see the town emerge from a radically different position than institutional discourse concerned with responsibility, compensation, or reconciliation at the state level, which operates within a distinct symbolic realm abstracted from embodied need.

This contrast is captured in the testimony of a parent of a second-generation victim: *"During the day I'm fine, but at night I start thinking, wondering what will happen to my children in the future... After I pass away... then there's nothing more that can be done"* (VN entry #. 20). The concern articulated here is not framed through the language of justice, demand, or compensation, but emerges from a site of existential vulnerability that resists political signification. It is not a symbolic claim for rights, but an unmediated expression of how Agent Orange is lived and endured, a discourse that cannot be absorbed by developmental or nationalist framings of state institutions. This disjunction reflects an epistemic incompatibility: victims speak from within a temporality shaped by Agent Orange, while official discourse remains confined to the symbolic register of policy, diplomacy, and development.

This epistemic incompatibility is further reinforced in official and institutional statements, where Agent Orange is framed not as a lived experience but as an object of governance. "*Agent Orange/dioxin victims have received great attention from the Party, State, and people of Vietnam with many specific policies and practical activities*" (entry #36). "*The government of Vietnam has made significant efforts to resolve the consequences of Agent Orange, emphasizing humanitarian cooperation*" (entry #31). These statements articulate the issue within a distinctly biopolitical mode of governance, in which, as Foucault (1978) argues, life becomes the object of political management through regulatory frameworks operating at the level of populations. Within this configuration, individual suffering is translated into administratively legible forms, organised through certification, policy intervention, and welfare provision, while the singularity of lived experience is subsumed under institutional classifications.

Rather than addressing victims as autonomous political subjects advancing individual claims, this discourse situates them within a population to be protected and managed in accordance with national priorities. Moral responsibility is expressed through standardised benefits, certification procedures, and institutional care, where compassion and obligation are articulated as functions of state coordination and collective administration. This reinforces a governing rationality that prioritises stability, cohesion, and developmental continuity in the postwar order.

Within institutional discourse, lived experience is routinely condensed through passive constructions such as "more than three million Vietnamese people were affected" or "have suffered," which position victims as statistical objects rather than speaking subjects. This pattern recurs across the discourses examined in this research. Linguistic and discursive devices consistently generate distinct epistemic frames corresponding to different discursive positions. For instance, the phrase "were affected" implies a closed and completed event, stripping suffering of its ongoing reality. Even "have suffered," though grammatically open-ended, avoids giving voice or agency to victims, confining them within an abstract category of victimhood. These formulations reflect an institutional mindset that manages harm through distance, record-keeping, and abstraction.

By contrast, when victims speak in their own voices, such as *"I was born without legs" or "I can't get married because I fear my children will be like me"* (entry # 1), the language is immediate, embodied, and relational. It does not merely describe suffering; it enacts it, allowing subjects to emerge through speech. Yet such expressions rarely enter dominant discourse, appearing only sporadically in qualitative studies. The critical discourse analysis demonstrates that across the dataset, this divergence in linguistic logic is systematic: although addressing the same issue, victims' speech and state or institutional rhetoric occupy fundamentally different discursive positions.

This divergence is further evident at the level of tone. Institutional statements are predominantly articulated in a forward-looking register, emphasising resilience, recovery, cooperation, strategic planning, and national development. The language frequently conveys optimism, progress, and collective capacity, framing Agent Orange within narratives of remediation, reconciliation, and inclusive growth. By contrast, first-person victim testimonies are more often characterised by expressions of pain, uncertainty, exhaustion, fear for future generations, and material precarity. Rather than projecting resolution, these accounts dwell in ongoing vulnerability and embodied suffering. This tonal asymmetry does not reflect a difference in factual reality but illustrates how distinct discursive positions structure emotional register, temporality, and the framing of responsibility within the broader field of meaning production.

The divergence between lived experience and institutional rhetoric becomes especially clear when individual testimony is placed alongside official statements. One veteran states, "*I have tried to seek help, but no one listens. I feel invisible*" (entry #4), articulating the absence of a recognised position from which his suffering can be heard. Yet government discourse asserts that "*The disability certification process is governed by criteria ensuring transparency, equity, and effective delivery of state benefits*" (entry #47), framing harm as administratively classified and fairly managed. Similarly, while a parent confesses, "*Sometimes I think it would be better if my son died… He suffers every day*" (entry #20), institutional language proclaims that "*The resilience of Agent Orange victims reflects the spirit of the*

Vietnamese people in overcoming historical hardship" (entry #40). In these juxtapositions, invisibility contrasts with transparency, and daily despair contrasts with national resilience. The government rhetoric converts ongoing suffering into narratives of procedural order and collective strength, whereas victims' speech reveals persistent pain that resists symbolic resolution. The gap is therefore not merely tonal but structural, exposing a disjunction between bureaucratic recognition and embodied reality.

Entries #75, #73, #69, and #66 explicitly embed Agent Orange within a developmentalist framework. Institutional discourse states that "*AO-related policies are aligned with SDGs, demonstrating Vietnam's progress on inclusive and equitable development*" (entry #75), that "*Integrating AO remediation with climate goals strengthens Vietnam's position as a responsible environmental actor*" (entry #73), and that "*AO remediation is integrated into the national master plan as a long-term development strategy*" (entry #69). Even more explicitly, "*Despite historical challenges, AO-affected regions have become models of economic resilience and development*" (entry #66). Across these formulations, Agent Orange is framed less as an unresolved site of individual suffering than as an issue to be incorporated into national planning, sustainability metrics, and international cooperation. In this configuration, historical trauma is absorbed within narratives of resilience, coordination, and forward-looking development. Suffering is thus symbolically contained within a developmental horizon rather than articulated as a site requiring substantive government intervention.

Victims' testimonies, however, register a radically different content. One parent states, *"Every time I see my son struggle to walk, I feel the war is still inside our house"* (entry #5). Another observes, *"They treat us like we're a burden, not part of the community"* (entry #28). Within the victim community itself, the phrase *"Di an xin"*, "go and beg" (entry #30) captures the humiliating social experience of having to perform victimhood in order to survive. None of these expressions, centred on shame, burden, and intimate domestic suffering, appear in institutional entries #66, #69, #73, or #75. The developmental vocabulary of resilience, strategy, and inclusive growth leaves no discursive space for the inner and relational dimensions of ongoing harm.

This is not to suggest that institutional discourse always diverges from victims' expressions or wording. Although rare, there are instances in which victims or their families articulate demands that appear to align with state language. In the same interview (Fox, 2024), the young man's father stated: *"The American imperialists who did this to us should compensate this."* While the content of this statement resembles official appeals for responsibility and compensation, it nonetheless remains outside the symbolic domain through which political claims acquire legitimacy and circulation. As Hammond notes (2024, p. 159), victims do not primarily seek reparation from the United States in the form of war compensation; rather, they seek acknowledgement that Agent Orange has caused lasting harm to the land and its people in Vietnam. It is therefore a demand, but one not registered within the language of diplomacy or institutional exchange. In this sense, even where semantic overlap exists, the discursive position from which victims speak remains distinct.

This divergence is also evident in how Vietnamese state-aligned institutions such as VAVA engage with the general public. VAVA's public awareness campaigns reveal a persistent symbolic gap. Rather than inviting members of the public to articulate their own concerns or interests, VAVA's approach presumes a passive audience. As noted in entry #77, *"We want to provoke pity, but from the pity they may become better motivated to help AO victims."* Here, the public is positioned not as a subject with its own interpretive standpoint, but as an affective instrument aligned with the institution's framing of the issue. There is no institutional structure through which these publics can speak for themselves or participate in shaping the discourse. Instead, they are positioned primarily as supporters whose role is to respond rather than to contribute.

It is also notable that Agent Orange victims in Vietnam rarely direct blame toward the Vietnamese government for its handling of the issue. In the dataset, none of the victims' narratives is critical of Vietnamese government policy or even suggests improvements or alternative approaches. Rather than viewing state policy as an object of critique or political debate, many victims appear to regard the government as the sole legitimate provider of care and support. This absence of overt criticism likely reflects a complex interplay of factors, including nationalism, a Confucian ethic of acceptance and endurance, political constraints on public expression, and deeply internalised state authority, even in the context of sustained personal suffering.

There are also practical and contextual factors that affect how victims' narratives register within the symbolic field. In field research settings, it is not uncommon for victims or their family members to struggle to clearly articulate their views. Encounters with foreign researchers, particularly when accompanied by local authorities, can be overwhelming and intimidating. Interviews conducted in the presence of large delegations often attract curious neighbours, further increasing discomfort. In many cases, interviewees are preselected by local authorities based on their perceived communicative ability. Even then, some may lack sufficient verbal skills or a clear understanding of the broader structural context of their victimhood, responding passively with brief or affirmative answers. It is also not unusual for visible pain and emotional distress to lead interviewers to shorten or discontinue interviews. Survivors of traumatic events often do not narrate their experiences in a linear or logically structured manner, further complicating efforts to render their accounts legible within formal research and institutional frameworks.

Theme 3: Biopolitics, Science, and the Management of Life

This section examines the biopolitical instrumentalisation of scientific and administrative authority within Agent Orange discourse. At the level of everyday experience, access to care and recognition is mediated through scientific and administrative classification within Agent Orange discourse. This authority becomes operative as a gatekeeping mechanism, structuring access to care and recognition within medical and bureaucratic systems. As one parent explains, "*We hope that our child can be recognised as a victim of Agent Orange so that when hospitalised, the financial burden on our family can be reduced*" (VN entry #10). This statement reveals how access to care is conditioned not on lived suffering itself, but on scientific classification and institutional recognition. Here, science functions less as a tool of justice than as a gatekeeping mechanism, translating harm into eligibility criteria and administrable categories. In doing so, it renders suffering legible to the state only insofar as it conforms to biomedical standards, while obscuring the political and moral dimensions of responsibility that remain unresolved.

The logic expressed in VN entry #10, where recognition as an Agent Orange victim becomes the condition for reduced medical costs, exemplifies how biopolitical governance operates through regimes of certification. This is consistent with Foucault's insight that truth is produced within discursive formations, where categorisation and classification render subjects legible and governable. Harm must be stabilised as a measurable fact before it can enter the circuits of institutional care (Foucault, 1978). At the macro level, global toxicological debates, largely shaped by US research institutions, structure the broader scientific field in which causality, exposure thresholds, and latency periods are defined. At the micro level, however, Vietnamese policy operates through a subjectivising relationship between the one-party state and the population, in which recognition is mediated by domestic administrative mechanisms, local discretion, political affiliation, and bureaucratic favouritism. Because care is organised around collective obligation, biological belonging, and national cohesion rather than individual rights, individual suffering is absorbed into broader narratives of unity and postwar development. Victims are thereby positioned less as political subjects capable of advancing claims than as objects of management within a population framework.

Within the Vietnamese context, Negri's account of cognitive capitalism helps illuminate how biopolitics operates through developmentalism rather than overt coercion (Negri, 1991; Hardt & Negri, 2009). Cognitive capitalism refers to a mode of production in which value is increasingly generated through knowledge, communication, and social cooperation, extending economic logic into everyday life. As economic growth, social stability, and national advancement become dominant priorities, life itself is organised in relation to productivity, participation, and contribution to the collective future. In this configuration, value is increasingly generated through the regulation of everyday life, social relations, and communicative practices, aligning with Negri's conception of biopower as embedded within the reproduction of life itself (Negri, 1991; Lemke, 2010). In this sense, cognitive capitalism can be understood as a contemporary extension of Foucault's concept of biopolitics, in which the management of life is increasingly integrated with economic production. At the same time, this configuration consolidates the conditions for biopolitical governance, as the regulation of life becomes increasingly aligned with economic rationalities and developmental priorities. Agent Orange victims, whose conditions often limit economic productivity and social mobility, are thus positioned at the edges of this biopolitical economy. While they are incorporated through mechanisms of care and welfare, they remain structurally excluded from the circuits of value that define contemporary life under cognitive capitalism. Their existence is acknowledged, but primarily as a site of management rather than as a locus of productive or political agency. This dynamic sharpens the differential valuation of life, normalising forms of exclusion and discrimination.

Within this intensified biopolitical configuration, the differential valuation of life becomes increasingly pronounced, bringing biopolitics into close proximity with racism and discrimination. As Foucault notes, once life becomes the object of political management, power determines which lives are protected and which are not (Foucault, 2003). Justified as the protection of the population, this logic produces hierarchies among human lives and normalises discrimination, a tendency intensified under capitalism and made visible during the COVID-19 pandemic, particularly through differential access to healthcare, vaccine distribution, and the prioritisation of certain populations over others (Butler, 2020; Lorenzini, 2021). These processes reveal how states increasingly govern through unequal valuations of life under biopolitical rationalities. Discrimination does not appear as formal exclusion, but emerges structurally through differential recognition: access to care becomes hierarchised through bureaucratic classifications that determine which forms of impairment qualify for recognition and which forms of suffering fall outside institutional eligibility. The result is a biopolitical order in which care is conditional, recognition contingent, and justice persistently deferred. This governing logic takes material form through a set of concrete administrative mechanisms.

Mechanisms such as disability certification, standardised rehabilitation protocols, and eligibility criteria for state support operate as concrete administrative devices within this biopolitical configuration. Official statements emphasise that "*The disability certification process is governed by criteria ensuring transparency, equity, and effective delivery of state benefits*" (entry # 47), and that "*Vietnamese victims of Agent Orange receive monthly allowances, free health insurance and free medical examinations and treatment*" (entry # 49). In this institutional register, victims' lived experiences are translated into the language of procedural fairness, benefit distribution, and regulatory compliance. These administrative mechanisms construct the discursive form of recognition; however, the content of victims' lived suffering exceeds this form, revealing a structural mismatch between bureaucratic classification and embodied experience.

In this process, the care and services provided by the state appear as forms of support, yet they simultaneously operate as mechanisms of regulation and differentiation. Within this process, victims are increasingly understood through technical and medical categories, which make their suffering easier for the state to manage but harder to express as political claims. This does not imply an absence of response; rather, attempts to alter their circumstances are constrained by a framework that lacks institutional channels for translating grievance into claims. Crucially, this positioning is sustained not solely by socialist governance, but by long-standing nationalist formations in which the state is imagined as the ultimate moral and material guarantor of survival. When the state functions as the final source of even minimal financial assistance, compliance is reproduced not primarily through coercion, but through dependence, gratitude, and the internalisation of obligation. This does not imply an absence of response; rather, attempts to alter their circumstances are constrained by a framework that lacks institutional channels for translating grievance into claims.

As one victim states, "*I was exposed to Agent Orange while serving in the army. My children were born with severe disabilities. I have tried to seek help, but no one listens. I feel invisible*" (entry #4). Another expresses resentment not as a formal legal demand, but as an affective awareness of injustice without a recognised site of articulation: "*I have a burning anger in my heart. The US government has paid compensation to US soldiers affected by Agent Orange, but Vietnamese victims have received nothing. The chemical manufacturers of Agent Orange have also never taken any responsibility for the suffering they have caused*" (entry #6). In this context, the absence of overt criticism directed at the Vietnamese state should not be interpreted as consent or satisfaction, but as the effect of a biopolitical formation that circumscribes the conditions under which dissent becomes intelligible.

As Althusser argues, individuals become subjects through the state's act of hailing, the process by which authority calls them into a recognised position. In this context, Agent Orange victims are hailed not as bearers of political rights, but as recipients of care and objects of intervention. This hailing, grounded in deeply internalised orientations toward authority, limits the space for contestation and narrows the conditions under which political agency can emerge. The Vietnamese state operates within a symbolic order in which it occupies the position of the recognised source of legitimate authority and official interpretation. From this position, its discourse carries authority even when it is partial or selective. The humanitarian, legal, and scientific vocabularies it deploys do not simply organise care; they define what counts as legitimate suffering and valid claims. In this way, the appearance of justice can coexist with the absence of full recognition. Medical and bureaucratic procedures further translate complex lived experiences into standardised data, replacing narrative expression with eligibility criteria. The result is not only a gap between governance and lived reality, but a continuing form of structural harm insofar as victims are denied the possibility of being seen and heard on their own terms.

"I carry the war in my flesh. Every day my body reminds me of what was done. And yet I am not only a victim, I am still fighting" (entry # 10). This testimony exposes the limits of biopolitics in recognising the full depth of human life. Rather than engaging life in its complexity, biopolitics reduces existence to a biological substrate through which political strategies are managed. Within this framework, hierarchical

distinctions emerge between normal and abnormal lives (Lemke, 2011), in which certain forms of life are valued over others (Edington & Lincoln, 2023). Such reductions help preserve the state's existing order, allowing unresolved issues such as wartime atrocities and failures of reconciliation to remain unaddressed. As a result, tensions arise where lived experiences of trauma, stress, marginalisation, and symbolic violence are displaced by depersonalised and state-centred interpretations. This disjunction creates a space in which victims are isolated not only from political recognition but also from wider publics, as community attitudes and the logics of international aid increasingly align with an epistemic order that privileges dominant narratives over embodied suffering. Agent Orange victims thus come to be positioned as burdens rather than assets within the prevailing structures of value.

As a result, victims of Agent Orange occupy a paradoxical position within social discourse: their suffering is central to national memory, yet continually deferred, marked as a wound too politically sensitive to fully acknowledge. This position sustains the fantasy of a unified, forward-moving Vietnam while structurally displacing what threatens to unsettle it. In this sense, the victims come to resemble Agamben's *homo sacer*: included within the nation's symbolic order only through exclusion, their lives simultaneously recognised and reduced to biological management. This zone of indistinction between *bios* and *zoē*, between care and control, constitutes the biopolitical reality within which Vietnamese Agent Orange victims are held.

Theme 4: Publics, Mediation, and the Failure of Narrative Circulation

An informal conversation with a Hanoi-based professional offers an illustrative glimpse into a widely circulating public attitude toward Agent Orange in Vietnam. The participant, a woman in her early forties, tertiary-educated and employed in the education sector, responded to the researcher's description of the project by remarking: *"We Vietnamese are future-oriented and do not dwell much on the past. It is sad that something like that happened during the war, but we can forgive and move forward."* When asked whether she believed Agent Orange victims shared this view, she paused briefly before replying: *"Yes, I think so. We are all Vietnamese. We have been through a lot in history, and now the country is developing and everyone is working together."* The response was delivered calmly and matter-of-factly, without visible emotional intensity, as though articulating an unquestioned social norm. While anecdotal, this exchange reflects a broader public orientation in which national resilience, forward-looking development, and collective endurance are prioritised, often at the expense of sustained engagement with unresolved historical events and the distinct experiences of Agent Orange victims.

What is required is not merely the collection of individual testimonies but the existence of mechanisms capable of translating these narratives into an open social agenda, within which different pathways toward recognition, accountability, or redress can be articulated and debated. Such mediation is typically provided by civil-society-based

NGOs and independent media. However, in the Vietnamese context, this intermediary function remains structurally weak. Although numerous NGOs are formally registered, their capacity for sustained public advocacy and rights-based representation is highly constrained.

Within this environment, the difficulty of building trauma victims' own narratives becomes apparent. Victims rarely possess the social, institutional, or discursive resources necessary to articulate their experiences independently or to translate them into forms capable of circulating beyond the private sphere. The development of a durable public narrative depends on stable interlocutors who can sustain long-term engagement. This reflects Žižek's broader argument, particularly in his engagement with Holocaust testimony, that traumatic experience does not spontaneously organise itself into narrative form but requires external mediation to become symbolically intelligible (Žižek, 2012). Yet in Vietnam, NGO mediation is frequently shaped by project cycles, funding priorities, and advocacy limits that do not fully align with victims' own needs. As one victim observes, "*NGOs come and go... it feels like we're part of a project, not people*" (entry #16). This remark reflects a pattern in which victims are incorporated into temporary initiatives rather than sustained relationships. Under such conditions, victims' narratives remain episodic rather than institutionally embedded: they are documented but not structurally integrated into dominant political or legal discourse. Consequently, lived experience struggles to move beyond humanitarian visibility and toward enduring recognition.

This narrowing of recognition becomes even clearer in the testimony of another victim: "*Sometimes I feel better after the physical therapy sessions, but they never talk to me about how I feel inside. It's like they only see my body, not me*" (entry #13). Rehabilitation is present, yet it is confined to physical symptoms. The distinction between "my body" and "me" reveals a fracture between biological treatment and subjective acknowledgment. Care operates at the level of physical management, while interior experience remains unaddressed. A similar pattern emerges in the account of a caregiver who notes, "*In a year, roughly 12 months, they had to go to the hospital 30 times, and each time there is only us to count on*" (entry #27). Institutional contact is frequent, but responsibility remains concentrated within the family. Together, these testimonies illustrate a configuration in which suffering is medically administered yet socially unrecognised. The body becomes visible to systems of care, while the person remains structurally peripheral, and endurance continues to be borne within intimate networks rather than translated into sustained political recognition.

This gap between biological management and narrative recognition is articulated explicitly by another participant: "*I myself, as a Vietnamese physician and victim of dioxin, have seen how many of our people carry not only the scars, but the silence. We treat the body, but who treats the memory?*" (entry #17). The question exposes a deeper imbalance between physical intervention and narrative processing, suggesting that recognition at the level of biology does not necessarily extend to memory, meaning, or public acknowledgment.

Taken together, these accounts point to a deeper misalignment between victims' lived realities and the communicative frameworks through which Agent Orange is publicly discussed. This gap is reflected in the disjunction between victims' everyday reality and the domains in which Agent Orange is publicly articulated. The contexts shaping victims' lives are marked by poverty, stigma, social isolation, dependence on medication, monthly support payments, and persistent fear. By contrast, the context underlying dominant Agent Orange discourse is framed around scientific evidence, lawsuits, trade relations, strategic partnerships, and USAID funding packages. These two contexts operate in largely separate realms, limiting the capacity for victims' experiences to be meaningfully translated into public discourse.

As one survivor, Mrs. Hồng (Fox, 2024, p. 142), insists, "*You must tell it, must put it into the pages of history. It must get into the pages of the history of our country, our generation, of the world to understand that the country of Viet Nam has people—men as well as women, old as well as young...*" This appeal expresses a desire not merely to be heard, but to be inscribed within collective historical memory. In terms of narrative identity, such inscription enables individuals to position themselves as characters within an unfolding historical plot rather than as isolated sufferers suspended outside meaningful time. As Ricoeur argues, narrative mediates between lived temporality and historical continuity, allowing subjects to configure disparate events into a coherent story through which agency, responsibility, and endurance acquire intelligible form. Memory, in this sense, is not simply recollection but narrative emplacement, a process through which one's life becomes part of a larger shared horizon of meaning. Yet this process remains largely unavailable to Vietnamese Agent Orange victims. Instead of being narratively positioned as historical agents, they encounter consolidated barriers to recognition. These barriers arise from entrenched cultural stigma surrounding disability, which legitimises discriminatory state biopolitics, and from an overriding ideology of national unity and economic development that frames Agent Orange as a managed legacy rather than an open political question. As a result, victims are prevented from developing stable narrative identities within the national story, leaving their suffering politically contained within the apparatus of governance rather than transformed through collective contestation.

This limitation of narrative inscription also operates temporally. War does not end with the cessation of violence but persists as trauma, identity, and social form. As Viet Thanh Nguyen (2017) argues, war memory in Vietnam continues to haunt the present, shaping subjectivities as individuals and communities attempt to reconcile personal loss with national narratives. Yet the capacity to sustain such memory is unevenly distributed. Cultural forms, literature, film, and media, play a decisive role in structuring how the past remains present. However, within a contemporary globalised media environment, memory is increasingly absorbed into a commercialised economy of representation. Historical experience is transformed into aesthetic and consumable forms, often oriented toward international audiences and marketable narratives. In this process, the articulation of lived suffering risks being subordinated to narrative coherence, symbolic effect, and global circulation.

Against this backdrop, the experiences of Agent Orange victims occupy a structurally marginal position. Their suffering persists across generations, yet cannot be fully integrated into public memory. As a result, their experiences remain neither fully acknowledged as past nor effectively incorporated into the present. What emerges is not simply a lack of representation, but a structural condition in which suffering remains visible yet cannot acquire durable narrative form or political force within the public sphere.

Neglected Dimensions in Agent Orange Issue

In closing the dataset analysis, three neglected dimensions warrant attention. First, the experiences of second-, third-, and emerging fourth-generation victims demonstrate that Agent Orange–related suffering cannot be confined to the moment of exposure or to a single generation, as intergenerational effects and delayed manifestations continue to shape lives decades after the war. Second, a gender-sensitive perspective is essential because Agent Orange–related suffering is lived through gendered bodies and social roles, with women often carrying disproportionate burdens as caregivers, mothers, and moral anchors of affected families, while their own embodied and emotional suffering remains secondary or invisible. Third, while this study focuses on Vietnam, the historical use of herbicides in Cambodia and Laos serves as a reminder that there exist even more marginalised populations whose suffering remains less documented, less recognised, and more politically peripheral. Their relative invisibility underscores how hierarchies of attention operate within global memory, where some victims become symbolically central while others remain largely forgotten.

Multi-generations of victims

When the act of making sense of one's own life is integral to everyday existence, the effects of Agent Orange are experienced differently by Vietnamese war veterans and by their offspring, who are born with severe health conditions yet have no lived relation to the war itself. For veterans, suffering is anchored in personal memory, wartime experience, and recognisable causal narratives. For second-, third-, and emerging fourth-generation victims [21], by contrast, harm is detached from direct historical experience and is therefore more difficult to articulate, explain, or situate within shared social understandings, both for the victims themselves and for the broader public.

This asymmetry is reflected in policy priorities. The remediation of the Da Nang Airport site, where Agent Orange was stored, has been treated as a matter of urgency by the US government, largely because ongoing contamination is recognised as a present risk carrying legal and political consequences. By contrast, the continuing manifestation

[21] According to VAVA, there are approximately 850,000 second-generation victims and 350,000 third-generation victims. Some literature also suggests the existence of a fourth generation (Cooper, 2016; Anderson & Taverna, 2020).

of Agent Orange–related suffering across subsequent generations has not generated a comparable level of discursive or institutional attention. Yet this multigenerational harm is no less ongoing. While soil contamination represents an environmental legacy of the war, the embodied consequences borne by descendants constitute a living and persistent continuation of that legacy. Although epidemiological and teratological research increasingly documents endocrine, reproductive, and neurological abnormalities among descendants, particularly affecting daughters and female caregivers (Vo, 2025), these findings remain marginal within official discourse in Vietnam. As a result, the symbolic and narrative frameworks necessary for recognising multi-generational victimhood remain underdeveloped, leaving affected individuals and families in a prolonged condition of social and political invisibility.

What emerges strongly from the dataset is the pervasive sense of remorse, guilt, and anxiety that parents feel toward their affected children. This is a dominant theme across the Vietnamese-language dataset, in which many respondents express deep fear regarding their children's future. The suffering described is not limited to physical disability experienced by children or parents, but is compounded by an underlying sense of hopelessness, often unspoken yet deeply debilitating. The largely silent suffering of multi-generational victims thus reflects not only biological exposure, but also the epistemic limits through which their lives are rendered intelligible within dominant Agent Orange narratives.

Entry #26, *"I am one of hundreds of thousands... born without legs and missing a hand,"* underscores the isolation experienced by second-generation victims. The speaker's phrasing suggests not only bodily difference but also a form of self-identification shaped through numerical reference rather than personal narrative. By describing himself as *"one of hundreds of thousands,"* the speaker situates his experience within a broader collective affected by Agent Orange, indicating how the issue is commonly framed in terms of scale. This quote reflects what multigenerational victimhood often entails in Vietnam, a biological inheritance of violence that remains difficult to articulate within established public frameworks. The missing limbs are not only markers of trauma but also reminders of how physical injury becomes the primary way such lives are recognised within public discourse. There remains no stable collective framework within the state's symbolic apparatus that consistently renders this subject legible as more than a recipient of care or a humanitarian figure.

Entry #20, *"Sometimes I think it would be better if my son died...,"* expresses a despair so intimate and devastating that it unsettles the moral frame surrounding caregiving. Unlike public narratives that celebrate parental sacrifice or perseverance, this statement gives voice to an honest and socially unspeakable thought that emerges from years of unrelieved burden, emotional exhaustion, and institutional neglect. It reveals the ethical and psychological limits of multigenerational caregiving, where the parent, most often the mother, becomes trapped in a prolonged state of emotional and material depletion. This sentiment does not indicate a lack of love, but rather the unbearable weight of sustaining a life that official discourse fails to meaningfully support or acknowledge. It exposes how biopolitical systems shift responsibility onto the family while offering little moral or symbolic language through which caregivers can express their suffering without shame.

Entry VN#15, "*When my father was alive, he said that heaven had already punished my two younger siblings… He feared that if he were to die first, only my mother and I (another surviving child with Agent Orange-related disability) would be left to suffer*" reveals how multigenerational harm is processed within the language of fate and family duty rather than public rights or institutional responsibility. The concern expressed is future care, but the framework remains domestic and moral: it is about who in the family will endure the burden, not about how the social or political system should guarantee long-term support. The suffering is thus interpreted through private obligation and theological explanation "*heaven had already punished*", rather than articulated as a claim that demands recognition. In this way, the quote illustrates how the consequences of Agent Orange extend beyond bodily impairment to reshape family roles, embedding responsibility within kinship structures instead of translating it into publicly recognised claims.

Entry VN#16, "*There are many nights when I cannot sleep and keep thinking about what I am supposed to do. My child is ill, lying in bed all the time, unaware of anything, and all daily activities depend on a wheelchair—it breaks my heart. Meanwhile, my own illness is getting worse day by day, my health growing weaker. I can only walk and do housework with one leg. I don't know what will happen later if I become bedridden or am no longer here... what would Hồng do then, who would take care of her? The more I think about it, the more hopeless I feel,"* illustrates the layered suffering of a caregiver who is himself chronically ill. His distress arises not only from his own physical deterioration, but also from the ongoing emotional strain of caring for a child who is entirely dependent. This is compounded by profound anxiety about the future, particularly the possibility of becoming incapacitated or dying before secure arrangements for his child's care can be ensured. The testimony captures how caregiving under conditions of long-term disability generates a form of suffering that is bodily, emotional, and temporal, structured by present exhaustion and uncertainty about what lies ahead.

Together, Entries #26, #20, VN#15, and VN#16 illuminate multiple, interlocking dimensions of multigenerational harm caused by Agent Orange. Entry #26 foregrounds the embodied subject of inherited trauma, rendered numerically visible yet narratively marginal. Entry #20 exposes the emotional breaking point of caregiving, where despair emerges not from lack of love but from prolonged exhaustion and limited institutional support. VN#15 articulates a tragic logic of care shaped by fear of abandonment and the absence of long-term security, while VN#16 reveals the compounded vulnerability of caregivers who themselves experience physical decline. Taken together, these testimonies demonstrate how harm is redistributed across bodies, generations, and temporal horizons, extending beyond those born with impairments to those who sustain life under persistent uncertainty. More significantly, they expose a structural gap within both domestic and international discourse: multigenerational suffering remains largely confined to the private sphere of family endurance rather than recognised as an ongoing public issue. Without sustained and urgent intervention in research on multigenerational effects, the persistence of Agent Orange–related harm risks remaining marginal to public awareness, remembered as a historical residue rather than a continuing condition.

Gender effects

The impact of war on women and children is well documented in conflict literature. Yet in the Vietnamese context, women's exposure to Agent Orange cannot be understood solely through the lens of civilian vulnerability. During the Vietnam War, women were not peripheral actors but central participants. As many as 1.5 million Vietnamese women took part in the armed forces, comprising up to 70 percent of youth volunteers, with at least 100,000 serving in combat roles (Taylor, 2021). Women were therefore directly exposed to sprayed environments, military logistics, and contaminated landscapes, making Agent Orange exposure a first-hand experience rather than merely an indirect consequence of war. Despite this, female veterans who later developed Agent Orange–related illnesses occupy a marginal position within dominant narratives, which continue to frame women primarily as passive victims or caregivers rather than as exposed combatants in their own right (Fox, 2024).

The gendered consequences of exposure are visible not only in participation during wartime but in its long-term bodily effects. As one woman states, *"I lost my ability to have children... something was stolen from me"* (entry #14). The loss described is not simply medical but tied to reproductive capacity and social expectations surrounding womanhood. Such testimony highlights how toxic exposure intersects with gendered identity, yet these reproductive consequences rarely receive sustained attention within institutional discourse, which tends to treat disability in generalised and gender-neutral terms.

Beyond direct exposure and reproductive harm, Agent Orange has reshaped the social and economic organisation of everyday life in gendered ways. While biomedical research documents sex-differentiated pathways of dioxin impact, women's disproportionate burden cannot be reduced to biological vulnerability alone. As McHugh (2011) demonstrates, women are positioned at the intersection of agricultural labour, domestic work, childbearing, and long-term caregiving for affected family members. Care frequently becomes full-time, unpaid labour, contributing to income loss, educational withdrawal among siblings, and deepening multidimensional poverty (Hammond, 2025; Song & Lê, 2023). This restructuring of dependency is evident in the testimony: *"My husband was exposed to Agent Orange during the war. Now my son is 18 years old, and he cannot speak or move. I have to carry him everywhere"* (entry #22). Here, exposure is historically linked to the male veteran, yet its enduring physical labour is borne by the mother. Agent Orange thus operates not only as a toxic agent but as a force that reorganises gendered labour and intergenerational dependency.

This redistribution of burden is further intensified by social stigma. Women associated with disability and congenital anomaly are often subject to moralised interpretations rooted in karmic belief systems, positioning them as responsible for misfortune rather than as victims of chemical warfare (D'Aquino, 2012; Myers, 2005). Such framings intersect with institutional discourses that treat "women" as a homogeneous category, obscuring how gender interacts with poverty, rural marginality, and disability (Song & Lê, 2023). As a result, female victims and caregivers are positioned simultaneously as biologically exposed, socially stigmatised, and structurally unsupported. Their labour sustains family and community life, yet remains peripheral within official discourse, which prioritises remediation, technical care, and national development. What emerges is not simply the marginalisation of women's suffering, but a gendered configuration of recognition in which women absorb the long-term consequences of chemical warfare without being fully acknowledged as political subjects.

Agent Orange victims in Cambodia and Laos

While this research centres on the silenced experiences of Agent Orange victims in Vietnam, it also serves as a necessary reminder of those affected beyond Vietnam's borders. Laos and Cambodia, despite sharing exposure to the same defoliation campaign along the Ho Chi

Minh Trail, have remained almost entirely absent from mainstream Agent Orange discourse. Their marginalisation reflects not a lack of harm, but their diminished strategic and political visibility within US wartime and postwar frameworks.

Both countries were subjected to herbicide spraying along critical segments of the Ho Chi Minh Trail that passed through their territory. Although the total volume of herbicides deployed in Laos, approximately 600,000 gallons, was significantly smaller than the roughly 19 million gallons sprayed over Vietnam, such comparisons obscure the intensity and concentration of exposure. Spraying in Laos was compressed in time and space, targeting narrow corridors of the trail and adjacent agricultural areas, with particularly heavy application over short periods. As contemporary reporting has noted, this represented an intensity of defoliation comparable to that experienced in major war zones in Vietnam at the time (Nguyen & Hughes, 2017).

Despite this shared history of exposure, postwar responses have diverged sharply. Vietnam and Laos have gradually developed bodies of epidemiological and health-related research addressing the long-term effects of herbicide spraying. Cambodia, by contrast, remains largely absent from both scientific inquiry and international remediation efforts. As the War Legacies Project observes, Cambodia has conducted little systematic research on the health consequences of herbicide exposure, and no epidemiological data currently exist for populations in previously sprayed areas (Agent Orange Record, n.d.).

This absence of data does not indicate an absence of harm, but rather a lack of institutional attention and resources.

The current US engagement in the region further illustrates this disparity. While disability-focused assistance programmes, such as USAID-supported initiatives in Vietnam and Laos, operate within a framework that avoids explicit recognition of Agent Orange responsibility, no comparable programmes exist in Cambodia, even in indirect form (Asia News Monitor, 2024). As a result, Cambodian victims remain doubly invisible: first through the absence of scientific documentation, and second through the lack of humanitarian or institutional acknowledgement.

This section does not attempt to provide a comprehensive analysis of Agent Orange's impact in Laos and Cambodia. Rather, it identifies their omission as a significant ethical and epistemic gap within the existing literature on Agent Orange. To acknowledge these victims is not to dilute the focus on Vietnam, but to recognise the broader geography of chemical warfare and the uneven ways in which suffering becomes visible, researched, and remembered. Their continued exclusion serves as a reminder that Agent Orange discourse remains incomplete so long as entire affected populations remain unnamed.

The Future of Agent Orange Issues

Any forward-looking consideration of Agent Orange must begin with an assessment of the structural conditions that continue to shape its political trajectory. The current trajectory of the United States, particularly under increasingly conservative administrations, makes a hardline position on Agent Orange predictable and ongoing. Denial of legal responsibility, reliance on scientific uncertainty, and resistance to symbolic admission of wrongdoing are not temporary obstacles but structural features of US policy. In this sense, the persistence of the Agent Orange deadlock is almost certain to continue.

One critical site of this shift lies in public perception. The limited awareness of Vietnamese Agent Orange victims among the US and global public has allowed political inaction to persist with minimal cost. Survey data from the 2009 *Attitudes of Americans on Agent*

Orange study (Belden Russonello & Stewart, 2009), which compared responses across generational and experiential cohorts, demonstrate that acknowledgment of responsibility increases with personal proximity to the Vietnam War. Veterans are most likely to express responsibility, followed by those who lived through the war era, while younger generations with no direct connection show markedly lower awareness. Importantly, the study suggests that awareness-building is most effective when it avoids accusatory or adversarial framing. This indicates that future change is more likely to emerge from gradual, relational forms of public engagement than from confrontational advocacy aimed at state actors.

Within this landscape, the younger generation in Vietnam represents a critical but underutilised conduit for reshaping how Agent Orange is perceived and communicated. Vietnamese youth have demonstrated high levels of engagement with global issues such as climate change and environmental justice, often through digitally mediated, cause-based communities that operate outside formal political structures. Equipped with social media literacy, transnational networks, and a strong orientation toward solidarity-based participation, younger Vietnamese are well positioned to translate local suffering into forms of narrative and engagement that resonate beyond national borders. Nurturing non-political, grassroots philanthropic spaces embedded within affected communities allows awareness to develop organically, grounded in proximity and care rather than accusation or spectacle. Such spaces create conditions for relational forms of attention and response, inviting participation through empathy and connection rather than moral pressure. In this sense, youth-led, community-based initiatives offer a viable pathway for sustaining long-term awareness and engagement with Agent Orange in ways that align with the gradual, non-adversarial modes of public consciousness-building suggested by existing survey evidence.

At the level of assistance, existing US-funded programs operate within practical and structural constraints. USAID-supported initiatives have often focused on rehabilitation services in urban or semi-urban settings, even though many of those most affected by Agent Orange reside in rural areas (Hammond, 2024). In cases of irreversible or intergenerational disability, rehabilitation alone may not address the broader social and psychological dimensions of harm. Practitioners such as Charles Bailey (2017) have therefore emphasised the value of more targeted service delivery, including home-based assistance, community capacity building, and public–private partnerships. Although a comprehensive assessment of current aid programming falls beyond the scope of this paper, future approaches would be significantly strengthened by incorporating sustained awareness-building and public advocacy components, ensuring that material assistance is accompanied by broader shifts in public understanding and recognition.

However, these improvements remain constrained by a deeper structural limitation. Assistance continues to be officially framed as support for people with disabilities "regardless of cause," reflecting the ongoing reluctance of the US government to recognise Agent Orange–

related harm as a distinct category. In the absence of such recognition, material assistance risks operating in isolation from the historical conditions that produced the injury. A future-oriented approach therefore requires a clearer separation between recognition and legal liability. Even without compensation or binding agreements, official acknowledgment of Agent Orange victimhood could have meaningful social effects. In the Vietnamese context, where disability is often interpreted through moral or karmic frameworks (Fox, 2007), recognition of wartime harm has the potential to reduce stigma and reshape community perceptions in ways that material assistance alone is unlikely to achieve. In this sense, the Consolidated Appropriations Act of 2023, in which aid recipients included specifically mentioned Agent Orange victims, signals a modest but meaningful shift toward more explicit recognition. Moving in this direction, by prioritising symbolic acknowledgment alongside material support, represents a more viable and ethically grounded path forward.

Finally, future strategies must broaden their understanding of harm. While environmental remediation, such as the clean-up of Agent Orange hotspots at sites like Bien Hoa airbase, has been prioritised due to ongoing exposure risks, far less attention has been paid to continuing psychological distress and the sustained suffering experienced by family members. These are not merely remnants of the past but ongoing forms of harm that remain open to meaningful intervention. Paying attention to these ongoing violations should carry a sense of urgency equal to that directed toward the remediation of dioxin residues at sites such as Bien Hoa. Addressing mental health deterioration and the long-term burdens borne by families should therefore be treated as an integral component of any forward-looking response.

In this reconfiguration, Agent Orange is no longer approached as a problem awaiting resolution, but as an enduring human condition requiring recognition, presence, and ethical engagement. The future of Agent Orange does not lie in the expectation of policy breakthroughs alone, but in a fundamental shift in how responsibility, assistance, and recognition are understood and enacted. From this perspective, the future of Agent Orange memory depends not only on legal or political intervention but also on cultural production. Artistic and narrative practices provide a comparatively safe and less overtly political space in which experiences that remain difficult to articulate within formal governance structures can nevertheless find expression. Through stories, films, literature, and visual art, the issue can be situated within shared temporal horizons, allowing it to enter collective understanding without immediately triggering political defensiveness. In this way, cultural work may sustain historical continuity and recognition where institutional discourse remains constrained, extending the field of responsibility beyond policy and into collective consciousness.

Conclusion

This research explains why a pervasive silence surrounds Agent Orange in Vietnam despite its scale and impact, arguing that across key political, institutional, and cultural domains, the issue is governed through a discursive configuration that privileges developmentalism, political pragmatism, and state-controlled forms of representation, producing epistemic injustice and sustained marginalisation of victims. The following findings address this question by examining how silence is structurally produced, maintained, and normalised across epistemic, economic, political, and symbolic domains.

Why Are Agent Orange Victims Denied Epistemic Recognition?

A cautious comparison can be drawn between Agent Orange victims and Holocaust victims. Setting aside debates over whether artistic or media representations can fully capture historical trauma, Holocaust survivor narratives function as enduring markers of collective human conscience, affirming that such violations carry lasting moral and historical consequences. Images of concentration camps, severely malnourished bodies, and gas chambers have acquired symbolic currency, serving as powerful reminders of events that must not be forgotten. This shared recognition enables Holocaust survivors to situate their suffering within a broader moral and historical framework, supporting processes of meaning-making over the course of their lives.

By contrast, Agent Orange victims have largely been denied comparable symbolic and discursive frameworks. Perpetrators have rejected not only responsibility but, through appeals to scientific causality, the very existence of Agent Orange victims, producing profound consequences for those affected, who are left without socially recognised frameworks through which to interpret their disabilities and life trajectories. While the United States denies responsibility, the Vietnamese state remains the primary source of support, resulting in a configuration that enables biopolitical control and limits the possibility of critical victim voices, generating a self-reinforcing cycle of subjugation. Most critically, this arrangement subjects multiple generations of Agent Orange victims to an ongoing violence of silence, a condition that demands urgent ethical attention.

How Does Developmentalism Shape the Recognition of Agent Orange Victimhood?

Agent Orange victimhood is shaped by the logic of modern capitalism, which recognises human lives only insofar as they can be incorporated into the endless pursuit of development and competition. Within

Vietnam, victimhood is rendered legible through a state-controlled symbolic apparatus that frames Agent Orange as a regrettable but concluded event in the history, subordinate to postcolonial national development, neoliberal economic agendas, and political pragmatism. Through this framing, a specific epistemic order emerges in which the issue is normalised as historical misfortune rather than sustained structural violence, enabling an assumed consensus to forget and move forward.

How Does Biopolitical Governance Produce Differential Valuation of Life?

Taken together, these patterns reveal a biopolitical logic in which lives are differentially valued according to their compatibility with developmental and geopolitical priorities. Within this configuration, Vietnamese Agent Orange victims are recognised primarily as objects of humanitarian care rather than as political subjects entitled to justice, while other categories of victims, particularly US veterans, have been incorporated into systems of compensation and institutional recognition. This differential incorporation produces a hierarchy of life in which some forms of suffering are rendered more previllaged, while others remain politically marginal. As a result, historical harm is absorbed into regimes of care and development, rather than confronted as a matter of responsibility or redress.

Why Does Recognition Fail to Produce Transformative Synthesis?

The persistence of silence surrounding Agent Orange can thus be understood as a failure of dialectical progression between form and content. The symbolic apparatus, operating as discursive form through institutions, policy, science, and development rhetoric, does not encounter victims' lived experiences as content capable of synthesis. Instead, ideology functions to arrest this movement. Operationalised through *objet petit a*, economic development is presented as a unifying horizon that promises future resolution while perpetually deferring recognition in the present. Within this developmentalist fantasy, victims are rendered intelligible only insofar as they can be incorporated into existing symbolic frameworks, as objects of care, rehabilitation, or sacrifice, rather than as agents of their own lives. As a result, their experiences are never synthesised within the symbolic order, and the dialectical process stalls, producing a stable form of recognition without transformation.

Why Does the Gap Between Lived Suffering and Symbolic Representation Persist?

At the core of this silence lies a persistent gap between the Real of lived suffering and the Symbolic frameworks that seek to organise it. The bodily damage, intergenerational trauma, and everyday precarity experienced by victims cannot be fully translated into the languages of policy, development, or humanitarian management. While the symbolic apparatus continues to produce coherence through scientific, political, and moral narratives, the Real of harm remains partially inassimilable, resisting complete integration. This unresolved gap does not disappear; rather, it is contained, reframed, or deferred within institutional discourse. As a result, victims inhabit a space in which their suffering is acknowledged yet never fully symbolised, leaving the structural disjunction between experience and representation intact.

Why does political dissensus not emerge?

The difficulty of aligning victim experiences with state and institutional discourse lies in the structural gap between governance and lived suffering. As political philosopher Jacques Rancière argues, politics does not arise from the smooth integration of voices but from dissensus, the moment when those without a recognised voice disrupt the existing distribution of the sensible. In Vietnam, where public discourse is tightly mediated through state-led and paternalistic frameworks, the absence of spaces for Agent Orange victims to articulate their experiences in raw, undistorted terms forecloses dissensus, rendering their suffering politically inaudible despite its pervasive presence in everyday life.

This research therefore raises a fundamental question: whether the dominant ways in which the Agent Orange issue is framed, presented, and perceived can be justified when examined from the standpoint of those who bear its consequences. When victims' lived experiences become the starting point rather than an object of mediation, symbolic signification is reversed, and the conditions for epistemic justice begin to emerge. Such a reversal does not merely offer an alternative perspective, but reconfigures the field itself, opening the possibility for ethical, political, and analytical responses grounded in recognition rather than management. Crucially, the harm associated with Agent Orange is not confined to the past. Psychological distress, social marginalisation, and intergenerational vulnerability continue to unfold in the present, binding multiple generations into a condition of suspended recognition. The ongoing violence of silence therefore renders the issue not one of historical closure, but of urgent ethical imperative.

Appendix

Agent Orange Dataset – Theme Table (Entries 1–80)

Entry No.	Quote	Empirical Theme	Analytical Category
1	I was born without legs and a withered hand. Maybe my children will be disabled like me. So I don't believe I can get married.	Intergenerational fear and social isolation	Embodied trauma and reproductive anxiety
2	I was born with severe disabilities due to Agent Orange. My greatest fear is that my children will inherit my suffering. I don't want them to live a life like mine	Intergenerational fear and social isolation	Intergenerational anxiety
3	I think the U.S. should pay compensation. The Americans should help those people who are still suffering from the war	Unacknowledged suffering and appeals for justice	Direct political claim-making
4	I was exposed to Agent Orange while serving in the army. My children were born with severe disabilities. I have tried to seek help, but no one listens. I feel invisible	Intergenerational suffering and societal neglect	Denial of victims' agency
5	Every time I see my son struggle to walk, I feel the war is still inside our house. They call it Agent Orange, but for us, it's the poison that never ended	Persistent domesticised trauma	Continuity of war within everyday life
6	I have a burning anger in my heart. The US government has paid compensation to US soldiers affected by Agent Orange, but Vietnamese victims have received nothing. The chemical manufacturers of Agent Orange, Dow Chemical and Monsanto, have also never taken any responsibility for the suffering they have caused.	Anger over unequal compensation and accountability	Victims' agency through moral indictment
7	When I met some families... (even) the normal child cannot get married. So we will suffer. Don't do anything	Social stigma and concealment	Constrained agency through strategic concealment
8	It makes no sense. Agent Orange came from the US — it was used here, and that makes us victims. A little support for people like us means a lot, but at the same time, it's the responsibility of the US.	Moral appeal to responsibility	Victims' agency through moral appeal
9	I look around and see my neighbors, my friends... Still waiting.	Ongoing neglect and deferred assistance	Suspended agency within structural abandonment
10	I carry the war in my flesh. Every day my body reminds me of what was done. And yet I am not only a victim—I am still fighting.	Embodied trauma and resistance	Victims' agency through self-assertive endurance
11	Even though my son cannot walk or speak, we still believe he is a blessing. We try to give him a life, even if the world ignores him.	Intergenerational caregiving and affective resilience	Victims' agency through affective re-signification
12	On stage, I dance to show what pain looks like when it moves. I do not need pity. I want people to see that we are still here.	Artistic self-representation	Victims' agency through performative visibility
13	Sometimes I feel better after the physical therapy sessions, but they never talk to me about how I feel inside. It's like they only see my body, not me.	Medical reduction of lived experience	Structural emotional erasure within medicalisation

14	I lost my ability to have children… something was stolen from me.	Reproductive loss and gendered pain	Biopolitical erasure of womanhood
15	We want the world to hear our voices, not just read about our pain.	Demand for narrative recognition	Victims' agency through discursive assertion
16	NGOs come and go. They say they're helping us, but sometimes it feels like we're part of a project, not people. When the funding stops, so does the support.	Instrumentalisation of victims by project-based aid	Humanitarian governance and the commodification of suffering
17	I myself, as a Vietnamese physician and victim of dioxin, have seen how many of our people carry not only the scars, but the silence. We treat the body, but who treats the memory?	Medical silence and unresolved memory	Memory, self-witnessing, structural erasure
18	So, I really hope the American people, together with the Vietnamese people, will demand that the American government not produce these chemicals any longer. Don't take them into any country. What is banned by international law should not be used. So stop using them. Yes… not just myself in particular, but the whole world in general opposes these chemicals.	Transnational Justice and Ethical Appeal	Victims' agency through global moral framing
19	I blamed myself for decades until I learned that *'the poison Agent Orange'* was the true culprit	Internalised blame and belated recognition	Epistemic injustice and politicised awareness
20	Sometimes I think it would be better if my son died. He suffers every day. He cannot move, cannot eat by himself. We have to do everything for him. If he dies, maybe he will be free.	Intergenerational burden and despair	Constrained autonomy within biopolitical containment
21	I spent five years in Quảng Trị during the war. My son was born early, and his bones are all bent now. He's twenty-two, but I don't think he will ever become a person. If we had known how poisonous Agent Orange was, we would have run away. But no one told us—not even the Americans knew.	Reproductive decisions shaped by familial and moral collectivity	Epistemic erasure and constrained reproductive agency
22	My husband was exposed to Agent Orange during the war. Now my son is 18 years old, and he cannot speak or move. I have to carry him everywhere	Multi-generational suffering and maternal caregiving burden	Gendered biopolitical labour
23	I cannot go anywhere by myself. I always need someone to help me. I cannot do anything like others can. I want to have a normal life, go to school, and get a job.	Aspiration for normal life	Constrained autonomy under structural limitation
24	They thought that my condition was a result of bad karma in my family.	Moral stigma and karmic attribution	Cultural moralisation of disability
25	We Vietnamese are victims. And also, there are victims from the US allied countries. And we all are victims, so we want to ask for justice, for compensation for us all, the victims.	Legal justice	Victims' agency through shared political identification
26	I am not unique, but am one of hundreds of thousands of people whose lives have been marked by our parents' or grandparents' exposure to Agent Orange. I was born as you see me, without legs and missing a hand.	Intergenerational impact	Inherited biopolitical injury and constrained autonomy
27	I mean, in a year—in roughly 12 months—they had to go to the hospital 30 times, and each time there is only us to count on.	Persistent institutional gaps	Structural neglect and familial dependency
28	They treat us like we're a burden, not part of the community. But we still try to raise our kids, to have a life	Social exclusion and resilience	Marginalisation within communal life

29	I came here and saw my country's pain... but not how we live with them.	Representation and erasure	Visual silencing, narrative exclusion
30	'Di an xin', 'go and beg' this is a joke among the community of victims	Performative victim identity	Instrumentalisation of victimhood
31	The government of Vietnam has made significant efforts to resolve the consequences of Agent Orange, emphasizing humanitarian cooperation.	Humanitarian state messaging	Diplomatic framing over victim-centered accountability
32	The dioxin remediation project in Da Nang is a symbol of reconciliation and scientific collaboration between the two nations.	Reconciliation through technocratic remediation	Technocratic and reconciliatory narrative
33	Over the past decade, the Ministry of Health has expanded rehabilitation services and vocational training to support Agent Orange victims.	Expansion of rehabilitation policy	Institutional self-legitimation and developmental framing
34	Legislation concerning Agent Orange compensation has focused on harmonizing national and provincial implementation of support measures.	Centralised coordination of compensation	Emphasis on administrative process over lived experience
35	The Government of Vietnam views addressing the consequences of Agent Orange as both a humanitarian imperative and a demonstration of national unity and resilience. Our comprehensive support system ensures inclusive development and long-term recovery for all affected citizens.	National unity through humanitarian narrative	Moral legitimation of state authority
36	Agent Orange/dioxin victims have received great attention from the Party, State, and people of Vietnam with many specific policies and practical activities	The state's moral obligation, benevolent guardianship	Political and moral justification
37	Thirty-five locations nationwide have been identified as requiring long-term environmental monitoring and remediation.	Technocratic voice as biopolitical tool	Data-centric discourse lacking human impact framing
38	Vietnam welcomes US cooperation in overcoming war legacy issues, including dioxin cleanup and public health assistance.	Bilateral cooperation discourse	Bilateral cooperation as geopolitical narrative
39	Promoting the rights of persons with disabilities affected by Agent Orange remains a core pillar of inclusive development strategies.	Disability rights inclusion discourse	Rights-based discourse within institutional framing
40	The resilience of Agent Orange victims reflects the spirit of the Vietnamese people in overcoming historical hardship.	Resilience as national virtue	Heroic national identity constructed through victim imagery
41	Educational materials now include historical sections on the consequences of Agent Orange to foster patriotism among students.	Nationalist educational incorporation	Instrumental use of AO history for nationalist education
42	These include characterizing Vietnamese as 'Agent Orange victims' when their health status or disability does not meet the criteria laid down by the Ministry of Health.	Positioning state-led victim care as evidence of global moral leadership	State control over recognition and eligibility
43	Agent Orange Day is a moment to remember the suffering of victims and reaffirm national solidarity in the face of foreign aggression.	Commemorative national solidarity	Collective memory reinforcing state unity
44	Vietnam considers overcoming the consequences of toxic chemicals left from the war, including Agent Orange, as one of the top priorities in its post-war reconstruction and national development strategy.	Development-priority framing	Historical trauma instrumentalized for national development narrative
45	We, as former soldiers, bear witness to the tragedy of Agent Orange and support continued national efforts toward recovery and healing.	Veteran solidarity narrative	Framing victimhood within patriotic military solidarity

46	The campaign aims to foster social responsibility by educating the public on the legacy of Agent Orange through uplifting stories.	State-directed awareness campaigns	Mediated optimism and narrative control
47	The disability certification process is governed by criteria ensuring transparency, equity, and effective delivery of state benefits.	Regulated disability certification	Bureaucratic framing of disability entitlements
48	ODA-funded programs for dioxin-affected areas demonstrate Vietnam's effective absorption capacity and partnership credibility.	ODA partnership performance	Aid performance over humanitarian impact
49	Vietnamese victims of Agent Orange receive monthly allowances, free health insurance and free medical examinations and treatment.	State-led welfare and institutional care for victims	Selective framing of care as evidence of responsiveness
50	The international dioxin forum showcased Vietnam's leadership in pioneering eco-remediation strategies, reaffirming its role as a regional model for post-war recovery.	International remediation leadership discourse	Moral and political self-legitimation through policy showcase
51	The rehabilitation center in Ba Vi has become a model for how local initiatives can improve the lives of Agent Orange victims.	Model rehabilitation centre narrative	Model framing emphasizing local initiative
52	Effective coordination among ministries ensures unified national efforts in dioxin remediation and victim support.	Institutional coordination framework	Efficiency narrative over responsiveness to victims
53	The State does everything it can, but the consequences are too massive. We are grateful for international support.	A narrative of insufficiency blended with diplomacy	Diplomatic moderation of structural limitation
54	Inclusion programs ensure that persons with disabilities, including AO-affected individuals, can fully participate in public life.	Generalised disability inclusion policy	Generalized inclusion masking unique AO needs
55	Our strategic roadmap focuses on sustainable remediation, health care access, and international collaboration.	Strategic remediation planning	Strategic language sanitizing historical accountability
56	The exhibition showcases the long-term effects of Agent Orange, emphasizing the resilience of the Vietnamese people.	Exhibition resilience narrative	Historical trauma framed through national pride
57	While we acknowledge the past, Vietnam chooses to focus on peace, reconciliation, and future cooperation with the United States.	Diplomatic perspective	Political softening of historical accountability
58	Collaborative efforts with international experts have led to new policy innovations addressing AO legacy issues.	Policy innovation through global partnership	Innovation discourse masking continuity of suffering
59	Several individuals were recognized for their contributions to overcoming the effects of Agent Orange in service of the nation.	Public recognition	Individual heroism overshadowing structural neglect
60	Youth participation in awareness campaigns fosters generational responsibility and national identity.	Youth mobilisation initiatives	Mobilisation of youth to reinforce official narratives
61	Businesses have contributed significantly to rehabilitation programs, reflecting the growing role of private sector responsibility.	Private sector rehabilitation involvement	Corporate responsibility discourse depoliticising structural accountability
62	Promoting international awareness of the AO legacy reinforces Vietnam's commitment to peace and global justice.	International awareness advocacy	Strategic global positioning through moral language
63	Scientific innovation must be linked to national development goals in addressing the impact of Agent Orange.	Science aligned with development goals	Alignment of science with national agenda
64	The series portrays stories of resilience and healing to inspire national pride and social cohesion.	Media resilience storytelling	Healing narrative reinforcing patriotic sentiment

65	Infrastructure and livelihoods have improved in AO-affected areas through targeted community development projects.	Community development improvements	Development framing masking structural violence
66	Despite historical challenges, AO-affected regions have become models of economic resilience and development.	Economic resilience framing	Resilience framing minimizing ongoing structural harm
67	Vietnamese AO victims are calling for the programme to be implemented.	Institutional framing; victim silencing, VAVA discourse; passivity	Filtered voice and constrained victim agency
68	Online platforms have helped amplify awareness of AO issues while celebrating national resilience.	Digital awareness initiatives	Visibility through state-aligned celebratory discourse
69	AO remediation is integrated into the national master plan as a long-term development strategy.	Integration into national planning	Technocratic absorption into state planning discourse
70	Modern Vietnamese literature reflects the enduring resilience of AO victims as symbols of national dignity.	Literary resilience portrayal	Literary portrayal reinforcing symbolic victimhood
71	State-funded films portray AO victims as embodiments of endurance, framing trauma within narratives of unity.	Cinematic endurance narrative	Cultural production reinforcing collective unity
72	The armed forces remain committed to supporting AO-affected communities as part of their ongoing service to the nation.	Military support messaging	Military benevolence framing within national duty narrative
73	Integrating AO remediation with climate goals strengthens Vietnam's position as a responsible environmental actor.	Environmental strategy	Linking AO to climate action for strategic legitimacy
74	Parliamentary oversight ensures transparency and equity in implementing AO-related programs and budgets.	Legislative oversight	Performance oversight reinforcing institutional credibility
75	AO-related policies are aligned with SDGs, demonstrating Vietnam's progress on inclusive and equitable development.	SDG alignment narrative	Framing AO within international development benchmarks
76	Agent Orange narratives are integrated into heritage projects to preserve national memory and educate future generations.	Heritage preservation framing	Heritage framing embedding trauma in patriotic memory
77	We want to provoke pity, but from the pity they may become better motivated to help AO victims	Instrumental victimhood	Emotional mobilisation for political legitimation
78	We honour the strength of AO victims and reaffirm our duty to turn suffering into resilience and national pride.	Presidential messaging	Transformation of victimhood into state virtue
79	Vietnam continues to call for international solidarity in addressing war legacy issues including Agent Orange.	Global solidarity appeals	Global call aligning with geopolitical positioning
80	Progress in decontaminating hotspots highlights Vietnam's scientific and institutional capacity to overcome historical challenges.	Remediation progress narrative	Progress narrative reinforcing state competence

Agent Orange Dataset – Source Table (Entries 1–80)

Entry No.	Title	Author(s)	Publisher	Date
1	Withered Futures: The Fear of Passing On Pain	Tran Thi Hoan	Testimony before the U.S. Congress	July 2010
2	60 Years of Damage from Agent Orange and Solidarity with the AO Victims	Pham The Minh	Testimony at Forum III	August 2021
3	They Should Pay: A Voice from the Ashes of War	Duc, Agent Orange victim	Journeyman Pictures documentary transcript	2006
4	No One Listens: A Life Lived in Silence	Mai Giang Vu	Testimony at the International People's Tribunal of Conscience in Paris	May 2009
5	My Son Still Fights the War I Survived	Lan, T.	VAVA Provincial Testimony Archive	March 2017
6	Agent Orange has given me a death sentence	Claire Colley	The Guardian	October 2017
7	Don't Do Anything: Marriage Stigma and Silencing	Hopton & Walton	Technical Communication Quarterly	2019
8	Agent Orange Twisted Her Limbs. The U.S. Is Abandoning a Vow to Help.	Ives, M.	The New York Times	May 2020
9	We're Still Waiting: A Village of Sickness and Structural Neglect	McHugh, N. A.	Feminist Epistemology and Philosophy of Science	2011
10	Public Statement	Tran To Nga	France 24	2021
11	Agent Orange Victims in Vietnam: Their Numbers, Experiences, Needs, and Sources of Support	United States Institute of Peace	United States Institute of Peace	September 2023
12	Agent Orange Bodies: Việt, Đức, and Transnational Narratives of Repair	Natalia Duong	Canadian Review of American Studies	November 2018
13	Experiences of children and youth with disabilities, and their families, from an Agent Orange affected rural region	Ngo, A. D., Brolan, C., Fitzgerald, L., Pham, V., & Phan, H.	Taylor & Francis	November 2012
14	Stolen Womanhood: Infertility and Grief	Geoffrey Cain	Washington Monthly	Jan/Feb 2010
15	AO Victims Speak Out	Bui, N.	VOV News	June 2013
16	Experiences of children and youth with disabilities, and their families, from an Agent Orange affected rural region	Ngo, A. D., Brolan, C., Fitzgerald, L., Pham, V., & Phan, H.	Taylor & Francis	November 2012
17	Interview with Dr. Lê Cao Đại	Dr. Lê Cao Đại	Texas Tech Oral History Archive	November 1999
18	Living with Agent Orange	Fox, D. N.	University of Massachusetts Press	2024
19	A Tale of Two Lawsuits	Phan Xuan Dung	The Diplomat	October 2022

20	One Significant Ghost: Agent Orange – Narratives of Trauma, Survival, and Responsibility	Fox, D. N.	PhD dissertation	2007
21	Haunting Images: A Cultural Account of Selective Reproduction in Vietnam	Gammeltoft, T. M.	University of California Press	2014
22	The impact of Agent Orange on third and fourth generation exposure victims	Vo, R.	The Stanford Journal of Science, Technology, and Society	2025
23	Delayed Reactions: 'Conjuring' Agent Orange in Twenty-First Century Vietnam	Uesugi, T.	PhD thesis	2016
24	The Start of the Crescendo	Tran Thi Hoan	Kent State University	Fall 2010
25	Vietnamese Victims demand accountability from US	Amy Goodman & Juan González	Democracy Now	December 2008
26	Agent Orange victim testifies to US Congress	Agency France Press (AFP)	Taipei Times	July 2010
27	Agent Orange: Consciousness and Conscience	Diane M. Fox	College of the Holy Cross	2009
28	Dioxin Remediation Technology and Risk Communication	Le Huu Dung	Journal of Environmental Technology	May 2017
29	Messages from the Heart (MA Thesis)	Blattenberger, P. A.	University of North Carolina at Charlotte	2016
30	"All Vietnamese men are brothers" Rhetorical strategies and community engagement practices used to support victims of Agent Orange	Walton, R., & Hopton, S. B.	Technical Communication, 65(3)	August 2018
31	Vietnam's Official Narrative on Agent Orange	Ministry of Foreign Affairs of Vietnam	Government White Paper	April 2018
32	Joint US-Vietnam Environmental Remediation Report	USAID and Vinh University	Joint Technical Briefing	October 2020
33	Official MOH Briefing on Victim Support Services	Vietnam Ministry of Health	Public Health Communiqué	December 2017
34	Legal Overview of Dioxin Response Programs	National Assembly Committee	Vietnam Legal Bulletin	June 2019
35	US Assistance to Vietnamese Families Impacted by Agent Orange	Hammond, S., & Đào Quang Toàn	United States Institute of Peace	2023
36	50 Years of Agent Orange/Dioxin Disaster in Vietnam	Ministry of National Defence	People's Army Publishing House	2020
37	Official Statistics on Dioxin-Affected Areas	General Statistics Office	Vietnam Environmental Report	January 2019
38	Vietnam-US Joint Statement on Post-War Recovery	Office of the Prime Minister	Official Government Release	May 2022
39	UNDP and Vietnam Policy Brief on Disability Rights	UNDP Vietnam	Policy Series on Inclusive Development	March 2020
40	Vietnam Television (VTV) Documentary Coverage	VTV Newsroom	Prime-Time News Feature	November 2021
41	Agent Orange Awareness in Vietnamese School Curricula	Ministry of Education and Training	Educational Policy Bulletin	February 2020
42	From Enemies to Partners	Le Ke Son & Charles R. Bailey	G. Anton Publishing, LLC	2019

43	Official Statement on Agent Orange Commemoration Day	Vietnam Fatherland Front	Commemorative Address Archive	August 2021
44	US Assistance to Vietnamese Families Impacted by Agent Orange	Hammond, S., & Đào Quang Toàn	United States Institute of Peace	2023
45	Vietnam Veterans Association Public Message	Vietnam Veterans Association	Veterans Solidarity Bulletin	June 2019
46	National Media Campaign on AO Awareness	Vietnam Television (VTV) and Ministry of Information	AO Awareness Initiative Report	April 2020
47	Legal Framework for Disability Certification	Ministry of Labour, Invalids and Social Affairs (MOLISA)	National Disability Law Brief	May 2019
48	Official Development Assistance in AO Projects	Ministry of Planning and Investment	ODA Performance Report	October 2021
49	Social security for dioxin victims is ensured	Ministry of Finance	International Social Security News	June 2024
50	Reporting on the 2022 International Dioxin Remediation Conference in Hanoi	Ministry of Natural Resources and Environment	Vietnam Plus and VTV4	September 2022
51	Local Television Coverage of AO Rehabilitation Success	Hanoi Broadcasting Corporation	Community Health Segment	July 2020
52	Inter-Ministerial Statement on AO Coordination	Office of the Government	Coordination Task Force Bulletin	April 2019
53	VAVA's Activities Supporting Agent Orange Victims	Vietnam Association for Victims of Agent Orange/Dioxin	VAVA Publications	2011
54	Disability Rights and Integration Program Overview	Ministry of Labour, Invalids and Social Affairs (MOLISA)	Disability Inclusion Update	October 2020
55	Strategic Plan for AO Legacy Management	Vietnam Environment Administration	Long-Term Strategy Document	February 2023
56	Public Exhibition on the History of Agent Orange	Vietnam Museum of War Remnants	Exhibition Catalog	September 2019
57	U.S.–Vietnam Comprehensive Partnership dialogue	Vietnamese Deputy Foreign Minister	Ministry of Foreign Affairs	July 2023
58	International Collaboration on AO Policy Innovation	Vietnam Academy of Science and Technology	International Policy Forum Brief	June 2020
59	State Recognition of AO Heroes	Office of the President	State Commendation Archive	April 2021
60	Youth Engagement in AO Awareness Campaigns	Ho Chi Minh Communist Youth Union	Youth Outreach Report	November 2022
61	Partnership with Private Sector in AO Rehabilitation	Vietnam Chamber of Commerce and Industry	Corporate Social Responsibility Report	March 2021
62	Vietnam's Strategic Communication on AO Abroad	Ministry of Foreign Affairs	Diplomatic Outreach Briefing	May 2022
63	Scientific Symposium on Dioxin and Development	Vietnam Science Association	Symposium Proceedings	September 2020
64	Television Series on Post-War Healing	Vietnam National Television (VTV)	Broadcasting Schedule Guide	August 2021
65	Community Development Projects in AO Zones	Ministry of Agriculture and Rural Development	Development Outcomes Report	December 2019

66	Government Media on AO Economic Resilience	Vietnam Economic Times	Economic Recovery Bulletin	February 2022
67	US Attitude is Softer on the Agent Orange Problem	Embassy Press Office	Embassy of the Socialist Republic of Vietnam in the United States	July 2010
68	Social Media Campaigns for AO Awareness	Vietnam Youth Union	Digital Outreach Summary	March 2020
69	AO Policy Integration in National Master Plan	Ministry of Planning and Investment	Master Plan Integration Memo	May 2021
70	AO Resilience Themes in National Literature	Vietnam Writers' Association	National Literary Journal	June 2019
71	AO Legacy in State-Sponsored Film	Vietnam Cinema Department	National Film Board Summary	April 2020
72	Military Perspective on AO Aftermath	People's Army Newspaper	Military Analysis Feature	August 2021
73	AO and National Environmental Strategy	Ministry of Natural Resources and Environment	Environmental Strategy Paper	February 2022
74	National Assembly AO Oversight Report	Standing Committee on Social Affairs	Parliamentary Review	October 2021
75	Policy Alignment with Sustainable Development Goals	Vietnam UN Partnership Framework	UN-Vietnam Cooperation Report	July 2020
76	AO Framing in National Heritage Promotion	Ministry of Culture, Sports and Tourism	Cultural Preservation Circular	September 2020
77	"All Vietnamese men are brothers" Rhetorical strategies and community engagement practices used to support victims of Agent Orange	Walton, R., & Hopton, S. B.	Technical Communication, 65(3)	August 2018
78	Presidential Message on National AO Day	Office of the President	Official State Broadcast	August 2022
79	MOFA Briefing on AO and Global Advocacy	Ministry of Foreign Affairs	Global Partnerships Bulletin	May 2023
80	Environmental Remediation Progress Report	Vietnam Environment Administration	National Environmental Recovery Report	December 2022

Vietnamese Language Dataset Source

Number	Quotation	Narrator	Source
1	I do not wish to live on compassion alone. I want to be able to act for myself, so that my child does not merely survive, but is also able to hold onto hope.	Nguyễn Văn Đức (father of a disabled child affected by Agent Orange)	Báo Nghệ An – "Nỗi đau da cam và trách nhiệm của chúng ta" ["The Pain of Agent Orange and Our Responsibility"], 10 August 2025, baonghean.vn
2	There were times when I believed myself to be strong… yet now, simply looking at my child lying silently, I find myself overcome by an unfamiliar sense of fragility.	Unnamed former soldier (father of a victim, Thanh Hóa)	Báo Thanh Hóa – "Nhân Ngày vì nạn nhân chất độc da cam Việt Nam (10/8): Nơi tình người làm dịu nỗi đau da cam" ["On Vietnam Day for Victims of Agent Orange (10 August): Where Human Compassion Soothes the Pain of Agent Orange"], 10 August 2025, baothanhhoa.vn
3	Putting everything aside, I still hold faith in the future. I taught myself a trade and make a living through my own effort and intelligence.	Lê Thái Bình (second-generation Agent Orange victim with limb impairment)	Báo Thanh Hóa – "Nạn nhân chất độc da cam tự 'lập trình' lại cuộc đời mình…" ["Agent Orange Victim 'Reprograms' His Own Life…"], 16 June 2025, baothanhhoa.vn
4	It was only after I married, had a child, and watched my child grow up with an incomplete physical form that I came to realise I had been exposed to Agent Orange and had passed its effects on to my child.	Unnamed mother (learned through medical examination that both she and her child were exposed to Agent Orange)	Điện tử Da Cam Việt Nam (VAVA) – "Chất độc da cam: Nỗi đau còn đó" ["Agent Orange: The Pain That Remains"], 28 August 2025, dientudacam.vn
5	I love my child deeply. When the ultrasound showed I was expecting a daughter, my joy was immense; yet when she was diagnosed with cerebral palsy, the pain was equally profound. I worry that when I am gone, there will be no one left to care for her.	Nguyễn Phùng Hưng (parent of a child with cerebral palsy linked to Agent Orange, Bình Phước)	Báo Quân khu 7 (QK7 Online) – "Nỗi đau da cam" ["The Pain of Agent Orange"], 29 November 2019, qdnd.vn
6	Every time I see my child gripping the pen to form each letter, his face twisted in pain, my heart aches for him. And when he finally manages to write, a new wave of worry begins…	Chị Thủy (mother of a child affected by Agent Orange)	VietNamNet – "Nghị lực phi thường của cô bé 8 tuổi…" ["The Extraordinary Resilience of an Eight-Year-Old Girl…"], 23 May 2013, vietnamnet.vn

7	Our family's income now depends entirely on the state allowance for Agent Orange victims and on a few small plots of farmland that we lease or lend out to others.	Nguyễn Thị Chế (mother of two children with Agent Orange–related disabilities, Hanoi)	VietNamNet – "Rơi nước mắt chuyện mẹ có 2 con nhiễm chất độc da cam" ["Tears Shed Over the Story of a Mother with Two Children Affected by Agent Orange"], 26 September 2016, vietnamnet.vn
8	I fought at the Quảng Trị Citadel and later settled in Điện Biên. My first two children were born healthy. Only later, when my son was born with a deformed arm, and then when my grandchild showed serious impairment, did we realise I had been exposed to Agent Orange. Every time I look at my grandchild, my heart feels as if it is being cut by a knife.	Nguyễn Văn H. (Vietnam War veteran, Quảng Trị Citadel; grandfather of a third-generation Agent Orange victim)	Sức Khỏe & Đời Sống – "Chăm sóc sức khỏe, đời sống để các nạn nhân chất độc da cam hòa nhập với cộng đồng" ["Providing Healthcare and Livelihood Support to Enable Agent Orange Victims to Integrate into the Community"], 6 August 2024, suckhoedoisong.vn
9	My husband, a direct victim of Agent Orange, suffers from many illnesses, and its effects have also passed to our children. Both depend entirely on others for daily care. Though often unwell myself, I must care for them every day; at times I am too exhausted to stand, yet thinking of my children makes it even harder.	Nguyễn Thị Tâm (wife of Lê Đình Nhạc, from an Agent Orange–affected family)	Điện tử Da Cam Việt Nam (VAVA) – "Thầm lặng trong nỗi đau da cam" ["Living in Silence Amid the Pain of Agent Orange"], 29 August 2025, dientudacam.vn
10	We hope that our child can be recognised as a victim of Agent Orange so that when hospitalised, the financial burden on our family can be reduced.	Đinh Mạnh Cường (grandfather of a third-generation Agent Orange–affected child; hearing-impaired and in poor health due to exposure)	Báo Hải Phòng – "Nạn nhân chất độc da cam thế hệ thứ 3, thứ 4 cần lắm một 'điểm tựa'" ["Third- and Fourth-Generation Agent Orange Victims Are in Urgent Need of Support"], 10 August 2024, baohaiphong.vn
11	During the day I'm fine, but at night I start thinking, wondering what will happen to my children in the future. That's why, while I'm still alive, whenever there is any good food or something special, I give it all to my children. After I pass away… then there's nothing more that can be done.	Unnamed elderly woman (suburban Hanoi; concerned about the future care of her children affected by Agent Orange/dioxin)	Điện tử Da Cam Việt Nam (VAVA) – "Nạn nhân chất độc da cam ở Việt Nam và nỗi lo về thế hệ tương lai" ["Agent Orange Victims in Vietnam and Concerns About Future Generations"], 23 March 2024, dientudacam.vn

12	After returning from the war, the greatest pain was seeing that my children and grandchildren were also affected by Agent Orange/dioxin and illness. I understood that once we stepped into the resistance, surviving at all was already a matter of fortune. Therefore, even carrying these pains within us, we soldiers had no other choice but to accept them and keep moving forward.	T.V. Đ. (Vietnam War veteran exposed to Agent Orange, Bến Lức District, Long An Province)	Báo Tiền Phong – "Lan tỏa tình thương và trách nhiệm vì nạn nhân chất độc da cam" ["Spreading Compassion and Responsibility Toward Agent Orange Victims"], 29 August 2024, tienphong.vn
13	It was only when our sixth daughter was born with many unusual signs that we realised we had been exposed to Agent Orange. She did not learn to walk until she was over three years old, and whenever she meets strangers or hears loud voices, she becomes frightened. Now she is over thirty, yet she remains childlike.	Vương Thị Quyên (Agent Orange–affected individual)	Dân Trí – "Nữ nạn nhân chất độc da cam chia sẻ câu chuyện cảm động trên tàu quốc tế" ["A Female Agent Orange Victim Shares Her Story on an International Train"], 1 May 2025, dantri.com.vn
14	Many nights I cannot sleep, worrying about my child, who lies in bed, unaware, dependent on a wheelchair. My own health is worsening—I can only walk and do housework with one leg. I fear what will happen if I become bedridden or die; who will take care of her then?	Trần Thị Hoan (Agent Orange victim with both legs amputated below the knees)	Sức Khỏe & Đời Sống – "Chăm sóc sức khỏe, đời sống để các nạn nhân chất độc da cam hòa nhập với cộng đồng" ["Providing Healthcare and Livelihood Support to Enable Agent Orange Victims to Integrate into the Community"], 6 August 2024, suckhoedoisong.vn
15	When my father was alive, he said that heaven had already punished my two younger siblings. Because they could not live as normal people, he hoped that they would die before him, so that he could remain alive to care for them. He feared that if he were to die first, only my mother and I would be left to suffer.	Lê Văn Ga (father of Lê Tấn Đạt, an Agent Orange victim)	Báo Tiền Giang – "Nghị lực vượt khó của chàng sinh viên nhiễm chất độc da cam" ["The Resilience of a Young Student Affected by Agent Orange"], 8 April 2024, txcailay.tiengiang.gov.vn
16	It's terribly hard. I am bedridden now, and the other four children don't understand anything at all. I love my children, but I am powerless to do anything for them.	Lê Xuân Chinh (Agent Orange–exposed veteran, Thanh Yên Commune, Điện Biên District; participated in the defence of the Quảng Trị Citadel in 1972)	Báo Điện Biên – "Chất độc màu da cam – nỗi đau bao giờ nguôi" ["Agent Orange – A Pain That Will Never End"], 9 August 2013, dienbientv.vn

17	Doctors say my organs are not in normal positions—my heart is central, and my stomach and kidneys function poorly. I travel monthly to Ho Chi Minh City for treatment, which costs 4–5 million VND each visit. The pain comes in waves; many nights I cannot sleep, but I have no choice but to live with it.	Trần Bá Nên (Agent Orange–exposed veteran, Thanh Hóa Province)	Điện tử Da Cam Việt Nam (VAVA) – "Người cựu binh bị nhiễm chất độc da cam, vẫn âm thầm đi tìm đồng đội" ["A Veteran Exposed to Agent Orange, Still Quietly Searching for His Comrades"], 29 March 2022, dientudacam.vn
18	We planned to have two children and raise them well, but each time a child was born, they died. After learning I had been exposed to Agent Orange, I realised that any child we had would either die or be born with deformities.	Lê Đình Nhạc and Nguyễn Thị Tâm (parents of four children, two with Agent Orange–related intellectual disabilities, Núi Trang Hamlet, Phù Ninh Commune)	Điện tử Da Cam Việt Nam (VAVA) – "Thầm lặng trong nỗi đau da cam" ["Living in Silence Amid the Pain of Agent Orange"], 29 August 2025, dientudacam.vn
19	When the weather changes, the pain becomes unbearable. My child suffers as I do, and watching this feels like being torn apart. I think back to the forests and streams we passed through as soldiers, never knowing they had been soaked with that cruel chemical.	Đinh Mạnh Cường (Agent Orange–affected individual, hearing-impaired and in poor health; family spanning second- and third-generation impacts)	Báo Hải Phòng – "Nạn nhân chất độc da cam thế hệ thứ 3, thứ 4 cần lắm một 'điểm tựa'" ["Third- and Fourth-Generation Victims of Agent Orange in Need of Support"], 10 August 2024, baohaiphong.vn
20	All four of them are slow and childlike like that. There is another one who is even more 'disturbed' than the others—he used to beat me badly, so I had to send him to live with an aunt in Nguyễn Phích commune to be looked after.	Trần Văn Đồng (parent of multiple children with disabilities, Bình Phước Province)	Báo Bình Phước – "Tất cả vì nạn nhân da cam" ["All for the Victims of Agent Orange"], 11 August 2024, baobinhphuoc.com.vn

Bibliography

Althusser, L. (1971). Ideology and ideological state apparatuses (Notes towards an investigation). In B. Brewster (Trans.), *Lenin and philosophy and other essays* (pp. 127–188). Monthly Review Press.

Anderson, A. C., & Taverna, M. S. (2020). The legacy of Agent Orange in Vietnam. *The Lancet Oncology*, *21*(6), 754–755. https://doi.org/10.1016/S1470-2045(20)30276-2

Agamben, G. (1998). *Homo sacer: Sovereign power and bare life* (D. Heller-Roazen, Trans.). Stanford University Press. (Original work published 1995)

Agent Orange Record. (n.d.). *Cambodia*. War Legacies Project. Retrieved July 14, 2025, from https://www.agentorangerecord.org/cambodia

Agent Orange Record. (2014). *Frequently asked questions*. War Legacies Project. https://www.agentorangerecord.org/frequently-asked-questions

Andrade, D., & Willbanks, J. (2006). CORDS/Phoenix: Counterinsurgency lessons from Vietnam for the future. *Military Review*, *86*(2), 9–23.

Arendt, H. (1958). *The human condition*. University of Chicago Press.

Asia News Monitor. (2024, December 20). *United States/Laos: US program helps victims of Agent Orange in southern Laos.* ProQuest.

Bailey, C. R. (2017). *From enemies to partners: Vietnam, the US and Agent Orange.* G. Anton Publishing.

Bayly, S. (2013). How to forge a creative student-citizen: Achieving the positive in today's Vietnam. *Modern Asian Studies, 48*(2), 493–523. https://doi.org/10.1017/S0026749X13000504

Bekkevold, J. I., Hansen, A., & Nordhaug, K. (2021, January 11). *The socialist market economy in China, Vietnam and Laos: A development model to embrace?* Developing Economics. https://developingeconomics.org/2021/01/11/the-socialist-market-economy-in-china-vietnam-and-laos-a-development-model-to-embrace/

Belden Russonello & Stewart. (2009). *Feeling responsible, acting humanitarian: Values that underlie support for addressing Agent Orange in Vietnam.* BRS.

Berry-Jester, A., & Murphy, B. (2025, March 17). *Trump halted an Agent Orange cleanup. That puts hundreds of thousands at risk for poisoning.* ProPublica. https://www.propublica.org/article/trump-halted-agent-orange-cleanup-dioxin-vietnam-poison-risk

Blattenberger, P. A. (2016). *Messages from the heart: Agent Orange and narrative conflict in contemporary Vietnam*(Doctoral dissertation). University of North Carolina at Charlotte. ProQuest Dissertations & Theses Global.

Butler, J. (2020, March 30). *Capitalism has its limits.* Verso Blog. https://www.versobooks.com/blogs/4603-capitalism-has-its-limits

Cane, J. (2010, January 1). Agent of influence: The realpolitik case for compensating Vietnam. *Washington Monthly.* https://washingtonmonthly.com/2010/01/01/agent-of-influence/

Center for Korean Legal Studies. (2022). *United Nations reports, statements and discussions on the "comfort women".* Columbia Law School.

https://kls.law.columbia.edu/content/united-nations-reports-statements-and-discussions-comfort-women

Chae, H. S. (2013, July 12). *Agent Orange lawsuit recognised—39 cases leaving further wound*. Channel A. https://www.ichannela.com/news/main/news_detailPage.do?publishId=56431051-1

Chizuko, U. (1999). The politics of memory: Nation, individual and self. *History and Memory*, *11*(2), 129–152.

Choi, Y. H. (2007). *The Vietnam War and Korean Army statistics* [통계로본 베트남전쟁과 한국군]. Department of Defence Press.

CIVICUS, VIDS, SNV, & UNDP. (2006). *The emerging civil society: An initial assessment of civil society in Vietnam*.

Communist Party of Vietnam. (1987). *Documents of the Sixth National Congress*. National Political Publishing House.

Communist Party of Vietnam. (2005). *Resolution No. 46-NQ/TW on the protection, care and promotion of people's health*. Party Central Committee.

Consolidated Appropriations Act, 2023, Pub. L. No. 117-103, 136 Stat. 49 (2022). https://www.congress.gov/117/plaws/publ103/PLAW-117publ103.pdf

Cooper, V. (2016). *Vietnam's toxic legacy* [Documentary]. Channel 4. https://www.youtube.com/watch?v=kMzJvwG2rsQ

Cutting, R. K., Phouc, T. H., Ballo, J. M., Benenson, M. W., & Evans, C. H. (1970). *Congenital malformations, hydatidiform moles and stillbirths in the Republic of Vietnam 1960–1969*. US Government Printing Office.

D'Aquino, A., d'Aquino, A., & Sutton, L. (2012). Agent Orange and narratives of suffering. *Occam's Razor*, *2*(5). https://cedar.wwu.edu/orwwu/vol2/iss1/5

Das, V. (2000). The act of witnessing: Violence, poisonous knowledge, and subjectivity. In V. Das, A. Kleinman, M. Ramphele, & P. Reynolds (Eds.), *Violence and subjectivity* (pp. 205–225). University of California Press.

Denzin, N. K., & Lincoln, Y. S. (2018). *The SAGE handbook of qualitative research* (5th ed.). Sage.

Diamond, L. (1994). Rethinking civil society: Toward democratic consolidation. *Journal of Democracy*, *5*(3), 4–17.

Do, T. (2021). *The future role of civil society in Vietnam.* https://thaongocdo.net/wp-content/uploads/2021/02/The-future-role-of-civil-society-in-Vietnam_Thao-Do.pdf

Dũng, P. X. (2022, October 17). Vietnamese war victims' struggle for justice: A tale of two lawsuits. *The Diplomat.*

Dũng, P. X. (2023). *Agent Orange victims in Vietnam: Their numbers, experiences, needs, and sources of support.* US Institute of Peace.

Dux, J., & Young, P. (1980). *Agent Orange: The bitter harvest.* Hodder and Stoughton.

Ebbighausen, R. (2015, May 27). *Vietnam's fight against hunger – a success story.* Deutsche Welle. https://www.dw.com/en/vietnams-fight-against-hunger-a-success-story/a-18477927

Edington, C., & Lincoln, M. (2023). Biopolitical Vietnam. *Journal of Vietnamese Studies*, *18*(1–2).

Esposito, R. (2008). *Bios: Biopolitics and philosophy.* University of Minnesota Press.

Foucault, M. (1978). *The history of sexuality, Vol. 1: An introduction* (R. Hurley, Trans.). Vintage Books.

Foucault, M. (2003). *Society must be defended: Lectures at the Collège de France, 1975–76.* Picador.

Fox, D. N. (2007). *One significant ghost: Agent Orange narratives of trauma, survival and responsibility* (Doctoral dissertation). University of Washington.

Fox, D. N. (2024). *Living with Agent Orange: Conversations in postwar Viet Nam.* University of Massachusetts Press.

Gammeltoft, T. M. (2014). *Haunting images: A cultural account of selective reproduction in Vietnam.* University of California Press.

Gao, Q., Evans, M., & Garfinkel, I. (2012). *Social benefits and income inequality in post-socialist China and Vietnam.* Oxford University Press.

Glaberson, W. (2004, August 8). Agent Orange, the next generation. *The New York Times.*

Goodkind, D. (1994). Abortion in Vietnam: Measurements, puzzles, and concerns. *Studies in Family Planning, 25*(6), 342–352.

Goscha, C. (2016). *The Penguin history of modern Vietnam.* Penguin Books.

Gough, M. (2002). *The political science of Agent Orange and dioxin.* Hoover Institution Press.

Grossheim, M. (2021). Reunification without reconciliation?: Social conflicts and integration in Vietnam after 1975. *The Politics of History and Memory in Vietnam.* https://doi.org/10.17326/jhsnu.78.2.202105.459

Gupta, A. (2012). *Red tape: Bureaucracy, structural violence, and poverty in India.* Duke University Press.

Hammond, S. (2025). Afterword. In D. N. Fox, *Living with Agent Orange: Conversations in postwar Viet Nam* (p. 154). University of Massachusetts Press.

Hannah, J. (2007). *Local non-government organization in Vietnam: Development, civil society and state-society relations* (Doctoral dissertation). University of Washington.

Hardt, M., & Negri, A. (2000). *Empire*. Harvard University Press.

Hardt, M., & Negri, A. (2009). *Commonwealth*. Harvard University Press.

Harriss, J. (2007). *Bringing politics back into poverty analysis: Why understanding social relations matters more for policy on chronic poverty than measurement*. Social Science Research Network. https://doi.org/10.2139/ssrn.1752973

Hayashi, H. (2015). Disputes in Japan over the Japanese military "comfort women" system. *Annals of the American Academy of Political and Social Science*, *617*(1), 123–132. https://doi.org/10.1177/0002716208327613

Hayton, B. (2010). *Vietnam: Rising dragon*. Yale University Press.

Hayton, B. (2014). *The South China Sea: The struggle for power in Asia*. Yale University Press.

Heidegger, M. (1962). *Being and time* (J. Macquarrie & E. Robinson, Trans.). Harper & Row. (Original work published 1927)

Heidegger, M. (1982). *The basic problems of phenomenology* (A. Hofstadter, Trans.). Indiana University Press. (Original work published 1975)

Hoang, B. T. (2006). Families of Agent Orange/dioxin victims of the third generation. *Anthropology Review*, *1*(8), 101–110.

Hopton, S. B., & Walton, R. (2018). One word of heart is worth three of talent. *Technical Communication Quarterly*, *28*(1), 39–53. https://doi.org/10.1080/10572252.2018.1530033

Jones, G. W. (1982). Population trends and policies in Vietnam. *Population and Development Review*, *8*(4), 783–810. https://doi.org/10.2307/1972473

Jung, M. S. (2017, June 15). Vietnam's criticism over President Moon—why? [베트남의 '문 대통령' 공개 비판… 왜]. *Hankook Ilbo*. https://www.hankookilbo.com/News/Read/201706151642400310

Kant, I. (2003). *Critique of pure reason* (M. Weigelt, Trans.). Penguin Classics.

Kandiyoti, D. (1999). Poverty in transition: An ethnographic critique of household surveys in post-Soviet Central Asia. *Development and Change*, *30*(3), 499–524.

Kerkvliet, B. (2011). The food problem in Hanoi during the subsidy period. *South East Asia Research*, *19*(1), 83–106.

Khong, D. (2006). Damaging effects of Agent Orange/dioxin: The pain of many communities, families and generations. *Anthropology Review*, *1*(8), 72–80.

Kierkegaard, S. (1980). *The concept of anxiety* (R. Thomte & A. B. Anderson, Trans.). Princeton University Press. (Original work published 1844)

Korinek, K., Loebach, P., & Teerawichitchainan, B. (2017). Physical and mental health consequences of war-related stressors. *Journal of Gerontology Series B*, *72*(6), 1090–1102.

Kurlantzick, J. (2010, June 16). Agent of influence: The case for compensating Vietnam's Agent Orange victims. *The New Republic*.

Lacan, J. (1994). *The four fundamental concepts of psychoanalysis* (J.-A. Miller, Ed.; A. Sheridan, Trans.). W. W. Norton. (Original work published 1973)

Lacan, J. (2007). *Écrits* (B. Fink, Trans.). W. W. Norton.

Lee, K. (2018). Is the progressive call for the government to apologise for the Vietnam War justified? [정부가 베트남전 사과하라"는 진보의 주장은 타당한가]. *Newstof.* https://www.newstof.com/news/articleView.html?idxno=1159

Lemke, T. (2010). From state biology to the government of life: Historical dimensions and contemporary perspectives of 'biopolitics'. *Journal of Classical Sociology*, *10*(4), 421–438. https://doi.org/10.1177/1468795X10385183

Lemke, T. (2011). *Biopolitics: An advanced introduction* (E. F. Trump, Trans.). NYU Press. (Original work published 2007)

Leung, S. (2024, January 12). *Solving Vietnam's social protection sustainability problem*. East Asia Forum. https://eastasiaforum.org/2024/01/12/solving-vietnams-social-protection-sustainability-problem/

Lewy, G. (1980). *America in Vietnam*. Oxford University Press.

Liesen, L. T., & Walsh, M. B. (2012). The competing meanings of "biopolitics" in political science. *Politics and the Life Sciences, 31*(1–2), 2–15. https://doi.org/10.2990/31_1-2_2

Lincoln, M. (2014). Tainted commons. *Medical Anthropology Quarterly*, *28*(3), 342–361. https://doi.org/10.1111/maq.12069

Lincoln, M. (2023). Biopower in transition. *Journal of Vietnamese Studies*, *18*(1–2).

Lindorff, D. (2010, January 1). *Media blackout on Agent Orange*. FAIR. https://fair.org/extra/media-blackout-on-agent-orange/

London, J. D. (2014). *Politics in contemporary Vietnam: Party, state, and authority relations*. Palgrave Macmillan.

Lorenzini, D. (2021). Biopolitics in the time of coronavirus. *Critical Inquiry*, *47*(S2), S40–S45. https://doi.org/10.1086/711432

Luong, H. V. (2003). *Postwar Vietnam: Dynamics of a transforming society*. Rowman & Littlefield.

Maclean, K. (2013). *The government of mistrust: Illegibility and bureaucratic power in socialist Vietnam*. University of Wisconsin Press.

Marr, D. G., & White, C. P. (1988). *Postwar Vietnam: Dilemmas in socialist development*. Cornell University Press.

Martin, M. F. (2012). *Vietnamese victims of Agent Orange and US–Vietnam relations*. Congressional Research Service. https://sgp.fas.org/crs/row/RL34761.pdf

McCulloch, J. (1984). *The politics of Agent Orange*. Heinemann.

McHugh, N. (2011). More than skin deep. In *Feminist epistemology and philosophy of science*. Springer. https://doi.org/10.1007/978-1-4020-6835-5_9

Myers, A. (2005, April 27). *Vietnam: 30 years later, war crimes go on and on*. Green Left. http://www.greenleft.org.au/node/32657

National Academy of Science. (1974). *The effects of herbicides in South Vietnam, Part A: Summary and conclusions*. USDA National Agricultural Library.

Negri, A. (1991). *Marx beyond Marx: Lessons on the Grundrisse*. Autonomedia.

Negri, A. (2008). *Reflections on empire*. Polity.

Nguyen, M. T. N. (2018). Vietnam's 'socialization' policy. *Economy and Society*, *47*(4), 627–647. https://doi.org/10.1080/03085147.2018.1544397

Nguyen, M. T. N., & Hughes, L. C. (2017, September 15). The forgotten victims of Agent Orange. *The New York Times*. https://www.nytimes.com/2017/09/15/opinion/agent-orange-vietnam-effects.html

Nguyễn, P. Q. M. (2021, April 30). America, please don't forget the victims of Agent Orange. *The New York Times*. https://www.nytimes.com/2021/04/30/opinion/sunday/agent-orange-vietnam-war-anniversary.html

Nguyen, D. L. (2022). Study on the participation of non-governmental organizations (NGOs) in local governance in Vietnam. *The Russian Journal of Vietnamese Studies*, *6*(3), 14–24.

Nhut, D. H. (2008, December 4). *Vietnamese Agent Orange victims demand accountability from US, chemical companies in suit* [Interview]. Democracy Now! https://www.democracynow.org/2008/12/4/vietnamese_agent_orange_victims_demand_accountability

Palmer, M. G. (2007). The case of Agent Orange. *Contemporary Southeast Asia*, *29*(1), 172–195.

Park, T. K. (2015). *The Vietnam War* [베트남전쟁]. Hanibook.

Parliament of Korea. (2023, June 16). *Special Act on the investigation into the war crimes against Vietnamese civilians during the Vietnam War by the Korean Army.* https://pal.assembly.go.kr/napal/search/lgsltpaSearch/view.do?lgsltPaId=PRC_A2Z3Z0H6G0G9F1F5D5E2A3Y2Z5X2Y2

Puar, J. K. (2017). *The right to maim: Debility, capacity, disability.* Duke University Press.

Ricoeur, P. (1984). *Time and narrative* (Vol. 1). University of Chicago Press.

Ricoeur, P. (1992). *Oneself as another* (K. Blamey, Trans.). University of Chicago Press.

Salemink, O., & Nguyen, T. A. (2019). The pursuit of happiness in Vietnam. In *Regimes of happiness: Comparative and historical studies* (pp. 201–218). Anthem Press. https://doi.org/10.2307/j.ctvdjrnx3.18

Schecter, A., Birnbaum, L., Ryan, J. J., & Constable, J. D. (2006). Dioxins: An overview of environmental research. *Environmental Research, 101*(3), 419–428.

Schuck, P. H. (1986). *Agent Orange on trial.* Harvard University Press.

Sidel, M. (2023, January 31). Vietnam's closing space for civil society. *USALI Perspectives, 3*(14). https://usali.org/usali-perspectives-blog/vietnams-closing-space-for-civil-society

Small, I. V. (2021). *US-Vietnam postwar reconciliation: A work in process.* ISEAS-Yusof Ishak Institute.

Soh, C. S. (2008). *The comfort women: Sexual violence and postcolonial memory in Korea and Japan.* University of Chicago Press.

Socialist Republic of Vietnam. (2002). *The comprehensive poverty reduction and growth strategy.* https://www.imf.org/external/np/prsp/2002/vnm/01/053102.pdf

Somit, A., & Peterson, S. (1998). Biopolitics after three decades. *British Journal of Political Science, 28*(3), 559–571.

Song, S. G. (2022, August 7). Why aren't Vietnamese more vocal about Agent Orange? *VN Express.* https://e.vnexpress.net/news/perspectives/why-aren-t-vietnamese-more-vocal-about-agent-orange-4489018.html

Song, S. G., & Lê, N. A. (2023). Inclusion of intersectionality and gender analysis in social policy development in Vietnam. *Vietnam Social Sciences Review*, (4), 42–60.

Song, S. S. (2018, June 10). Is there regionalism in Vietnam too? *Women News.* https://www.womennews.co.kr/news/articleView.html?idxno=142564

Stanford Encyclopedia of Philosophy. (2025, February 16). *Paul Ricoeur.* https://plato.stanford.edu/entries/ricoeur/

Steinman, R. (2021, August 1). *The media's failure on Agent Orange.* History News Network. https://historynewsnetwork.org/article/the-medias-failure-on-agent-orange

Tan, C. (2011). The new biopower. *Third World Quarterly, 32*(6), 1039–1056.

Taylor, S. C. (2021, October 24). *The women who won the Vietnam War.* History News Network. https://historynewsnetwork.org/article/the-women-who-won-the-vietnam-war

Trooboff, P. D. (1975). *Law and responsibility in warfare, the Vietnam experience.* University of North Carolina Press.

Turley, W. S., & Selden, M. (1993). *Reinventing Vietnamese socialism.* Routledge.

UNFPA. (2021). *Vietnam abortion statistics report.* United Nations Population Fund. https://vietnam.unfpa.org/sites/default/files/pub-pdf/info3_abortion_2_pages.pdf

USAID. (2019). *Disability program factsheet: Vietnam.* https://www.usaid.gov/sites/default/files/2022-05/Disability_USIP_-_factsheet_2019_Eng.pdf

US Institute of Peace. (2022). *Addressing the harmful legacy of Agent Orange in Vietnam*. https://www.usip.org/publications/2022/01/addressing-harmful-legacy-agent-orange-vietnam

US professor urges Vietnamese agent orange victims to raise voice. (2004, May 23). *BBC Monitoring Asia Pacific*.

Uesugi, T. (2011). *Delayed reactions: 'Conjuring' Agent Orange in twenty-first century Vietnam*. McGill University.

VA Claims Insider. (2023, June 12). *The complete list of Agent Orange presumptive conditions*. https://vaclaimsinsider.com/agent-orange-presumptive-conditions-list/

Viet Thanh Nguyen. (2017). *Nothing ever dies: Vietnam and the memories of war*. Harvard University Press.

Vietnam Union of Friendship Organizations. (n.d.). *Committee for Foreign Non-Governmental Organization Affairs (COMINGO)*. https://www.ngocentre.org.vn/comingo-vufo-and-paccom

Vietnam.vn. (n.d.). *Enhancing the effectiveness of mobilizing foreign non-governmental aid* [Nâng cao hiệu quả vận động viện trợ phi chính phủ nước ngoài]. https://www.vietnam.vn/en/nang-cao-hieu-qua-van-dong-vien-tro-phi-chinh-phu-nuoc-ngoai

VNExpress. (2023, February 7). *S. Korea court orders gov't to compensate Vietnam massacre victim*. VNExpress International. https://e.vnexpress.net/news/news/s-korea-court-orders-gov-t-to-compensate-vietnam-massacre-victim-4567841.html

Vo, R. (2025). The impact of Agent Orange on third and fourth generation exposure victims. *Intersect: The Stanford Journal of Science, Technology, and Society, 18*(2).

Vo, V. T., & Hoang, X. S. (2023). [Title of Article]. *International Journal of Social Science and Human Research, 6*(2). https://doi.org/10.47191/ijsshr/v6-i2-28

Walton, R., & Hopton, S. B. (2018). "All Vietnamese men are brothers": Rhetorical strategies and community engagement practices used to support victims of Agent Orange. *Technical Communication*, *65*(3), 309–325.

Weheliye, A. G. (2014). *Habeas viscus: Racializing assemblages, biopolitics, and black feminist theories of the human*. Duke University Press.

World Health Organization. (2010). *Dioxins and their effects on human health*. WHO Fact Sheet No. 225.

World Bank. (2023). *Poverty headcount ratio at national poverty lines (% of population) – Vietnam*. https://data.worldbank.org/indicator/SI.POV.NAHC?locations=VN

Wolfle, D. (1989). *Renewing a scientific society: The American Association for the Advancement of Science from World War II to 1970*. AAAS.

Young, A. L., & Reggiani, G. M. (Eds.). (1988). *Agent Orange and its associated dioxin: Assessment of a controversy*. Elsevier.

Žižek, S. (1989). *The sublime object of ideology*. Verso.

Žižek, S. (2012). *Less than nothing: Hegel and the shadow of dialectical materialism*. Verso.

Index

D

E

About the Author

Se Gun Song is a Sydney-based researcher. His research interests include biopolitics, critical discourse analysis of war victim narratives in Vietnam, refugee studies, and the Australian multiculturalism.

www.ingramcontent.com/pod-product-compliance
Lightning Source LLC
LaVergne TN
LVHW050957080826
845145LV00009B/2332

* 9 7 8 1 7 6 4 5 7 1 8 0 7 *